Contents

Photos courtesy of:
Aquarium Products; Dr. Herbert R. Axelrod; George Dibley; Dr.
Guido Dingerkus; F. J. Dodd, Jr.; Dr. Burt Frank; Michael Gilroy;
B. Kahl; J. K. Langhammer; Charles O. Masters; W. Mudrack;
Aaron Norman; Barry Pengilley; Penn-Plax, Inc.; Mervin F. Rob-
erts; Wardley Products, Fred Rosenzweig.
With special thanks to Kodansha, Ltd.

SECOND EDITION

© 1987 by T.F.H. Publications, Inc.

Distributed in the UNITED STATES by T.F.H. Publications, Inc., 211 West Sylvania
Avenue, Neptune City, NJ 07753; in CANADA to the Pet Trade by H & L Pet Sup-
plies Inc., 27 Kingston Crescent, Kitchener, Ontario N2B 2T6; Rolf C. Hagen Ltd.,
3225 Sartelon Street, Montreal 382 Quebec; in CANADA to the Book Trade by
Macmillan of Canada (A Division of Canada Publishing Corporation), 164 Com-
mander Boulevard, Agincourt, Ontario M1S 3C7; in ENGLAND by T.F.H. Publica-
tions Limited, 4 Kier Park, Ascot, Berkshire SL5 7DS; in AUSTRALIA AND THE
SOUTH PACIFIC by T.F.H. (Australia) Pty. Ltd., Box 149, Brookvale 2100 N.S.W.,
Australia; in NEW ZEALAND by Ross Haines & Son, Ltd., 18 Monmouth Street,
Grey Lynn, Auckland 2 New Zealand; in SINGAPORE AND MALAYSIA by MPH
Distributors (S) Pte., Ltd., 601 Sims Drive, #03/07/21, Singapore 1438; in the
PHILIPPINES by Bio-Research, 5 Lippay Street, San Lorenzo Village, Makati Rizal;
in SOUTH AFRICA by Multipet Pty. Ltd., 30 Turners Avenue, Durban 4001. Pub-
lished by T.F.H. Publications Inc. Manufactured in the United States of America
by T.F.H. Publications, Inc.

A COMPLETE INTRODUCTION TO
KOI
AND GARDEN POOLS

Dr. Herbert R. Axelrod

The author's wife feeding koi from her hand. Mrs. Axelrod raised these fish
from the first spawning in the koi pond at their home in New Jersey. The
pond freezes almost solid in the winter.

Introduction

During my two-year stay in Japan, I had the honor and privilege of meeting the royal family, fishing with Emperor Hirohito in Sagami Bay, and cruising the Palace grounds in Tokyo where the moat and the ponds all contained Japanese colored carp or "koi," as they are referred to in Japanese.

During the years following that stay (1950-1952) I retained my interest in koi. When I operated a fish farm in Florida, I brought in many thousands of koi from Japan and started breeding koi for the first time in any warm climate. Eventually those koi were the seed stock for koi bred in England and many other parts of the western world, and they were introduced slowly to aquarium shops throughout Europe and the Western Hemisphere.

Today colored carp are to be found in more outdoor ponds than are goldfish because they are larger, become tamer, are more colorful, and can be eaten when they become too big. After all, Japanese colored carp are nothing more than the ordinary carp (which is a major food fish in Israel and many of the eastern European countries) that has been selectively inbred for color and finnage. Long-finned koi are a 1986 development, though individual specimens did show up throughout the 35 years that I have kept them as pets.

When the peoples of eastern Europe immigrated to America, they brought carp with them. These carp were introduced into the natural waters of the mid-Atlantic states in America and are now considered as "normal" fauna of the area. It is doubtful that any of the American

Typical European mirror carp that are raised for food in eastern Europe. The Japanese have introduced this strain into the fancy colored koi and have produced many interesting color variations as you will be able to observe further on in this book.

These types of carps, the scaled and the scaleless, have been introduced into temperate waters all over the world. Anglers catch them regularly in most parts of Europe and the eastern United States.

continental states are free of carp. As more and more are caught on hook-and-line they are slowly finding their way into the American diet, for they are extremely tasty. Added to this is the fact that they are very hardy and can live for hours in a crowded bucket of water . . . which makes them the freshest fish that almost anyone can eat!

Today koi are to be found in most aquarium shops, especially in the spring of the year when most shops carry garden pool fishes and accessories. While prize specimens are worth thousands of dollars, you are best advised to leave the larger ones to the breeders and buy smaller ones 3 to 6 inches in length. Though colors change when the koi get larger, they still have a chance of becoming very colorful and are much less expensive than the larger fish. Well-fed koi in a properly filtered and aerated garden pool (the filtering and aeration are usually

accomplished with water changers or swimming pool filters) grow in direct proportion to their being adequately fed. If you offer live foods and proper koi pond food, you can expect three or more inches of growth per year. Though I personally use Wardley's koi food, there are probably other brands that are just as nutritious, but Wardley's floats. For some reason the koi become tamer on floating food and within a few weeks begin to eat out of my hand!

You should buy your koi through your local pet shop as you will need to visit it from time to time for help in solving your technical and health problems. While Woolworth's might sell koi, it is doubtful that they have anything else (including knowledgeable sales people) to help you achieve success with your garden pool.

Koi also make nice aquarium fish. I have a 10,000-gallon garden pool in which I keep my breeders, but many of the younger koi, especially the long-finned ones, are maintained in 200-gallon tanks in my office waiting room. They are extremely hardy and easily survive 6 inches of ice on the pool in the winter. The few problems I have take place during

The author has fed his koi Wardley's koi food because it floats and is a balanced diet. In the 15 years he has kept the same koi, no other manufactured or living foods have been purposely introduced into the pond.

the summer, when lack of rain and lots of sun combine to make an algal bloom that reduces the oxygen content of the water and stresses the koi. However, after more than 20 years of keeping koi in the same pool, I have never had a disease that killed more than a few fish . . . even when I was away for a month at a time and no one cared for them!

While koi are very hardy and can live under almost unbearable (for other fishes) conditions, they only thrive and show off their best colors and behavior when they are properly managed. This book will tell you how to easily care for them, breed them, and recognize the color varieties. Unfortunately, the Japanese nomenclature has prevailed when it comes to identifying koi . . . but they use American nomenclature when they play baseball, so I guess we're even!

Since koi are heavy eaters, they require lots of filtration and aeration if they are to be maintained in aquariums. The diagram below shows the path of the water in a typical undergravel filter system. Half the sand has been cut away in the drawing to show the water being sucked through the gravel and into an airlift tube that helps aerate the cleaned water.

Koi as an Ancient Hobby

There are animals with backbones and animals without backbones. Those without backbones are called invertebrates; those with backbones are referred to as vertebrates. The vertebrate animals include humans and koi. The invertebrates far outnumber the vertebrates in species, and there are more insects in the world than all other groups of vertebrates and invertebrates combined. Fishes include the richest variety of the vertebrates, with about 20-30,000 different species. Why such a spread . . . 10,000 species? It is certainly agreed by all scientists that not every fish is known to science and has been described in an appropriate journal, magazine, or book. But as a matter of fact, scientists who study fishes, called ichthyologists, hardly agree on the definition of what is a species or subspecies. Thus what one ichthyologist calls a species may be what another ichthyologist calls a subspecies of another species. Those ichthyologists who look for differences between specimens that are closely related to one another are called "splitters," while those ichthyologists who look for similarities between such specimens are called "lumpers." It is estimated that lumpers recognize approximately 20,000

Terraced undergravel filters are often difficult to find. They were invented by the author to give 50% more filtering surface and terracing, but they didn't find commercial support. Terracing is necessary to bring the debris to one accessible area from which it may be siphoned.

fish species, while splitters recognize some 30,000. It is not anticipated that lumpers and splitters will ever reconcile their differences.

During the hundreds of millions of years that the Earth has been developing as the only "living" planet thus far discovered, fishes at one time outnumbered all other living vertebrates ten to one! The fossil record, in which the author is very interested, has demonstrated that evolved (indirectly of course) from fishes. Think for a moment about unborn babies . . . they breathe and live in an aquatic environment. While Man is a vertebrate, he is also a mammal. All mammals are vertebrates, but not all vertebrates are mammals. Fishes are not mammals. Mammals are distinguished, in general, by the way they feed their young (by suckling). Yet fishes and mammals have much in common: They both have skin,

Your koi pond can be a truly fascinating experience. It will ultimately contain dozens of living forms other than fishes as you will discover by reading this book thoroughly.

fishes evolved into many sizes and shapes. Many would have us believe that since the Earth was first completely covered with water and since fossils of fishes are known from millions of years before Man, Man must have scales (hair), livers, kidneys, muscles, cartilage and bones, spleens, stomachs, eyes, etc. These organs that they have in common add evidence that Man and fish are related.

The great Japanese painter Utamaro painted this many years ago. It is called "Koi in Nishiki-e."

Life on Earth

Scientists disagree on both the age of the Earth and the way it was formed. Almost all agree, however, that the Sun erupted in some way and gave birth to at least the inner planets—Mercury, Venus, Earth, Mars, Jupiter, and Saturn. These are the major planets that revolve around our sun, and they have been listed in their order of distance from the Sun, with Mercury being closest. The outer planets (Uranus, Neptune, and Pluto) are of more uncertain origin and may be escaped moons or even captured comets.

Above: A Doitsu Shiromuji Ohgon, which is a German white metallic carp. Below: Most carps breed at random in typical situations, therefore their progeny are unpredictable in terms of color.

It is generally accepted that the earth was formed some four billion years or more ago, but there is no consensus about *how* the Earth was formed. Perhaps two giant stars (our Sun is a star) collided and giant particles flew off to become planets of our Sun; or perhaps there was just a near miss and the forces of gravity

tore off chunks of the Sun; or perhaps there was so much solar dust surrounding the Sun that it coalesced into lumps. The fact that the center of the Earth is molten and very hot seems to support the "collision" or "near miss" theory, but it is a far from simple question.

It probably took over a billion years of earthy formation and processing before the first living things appeared on Earth. These were single-celled plants soon followed by simple animals.

fishes with bony plates because it is basically the bones that fossilize and hold the fossil record together. Sharks, for example, have no bones, except for their teeth, which, like elephant tusks, preserve easily in the fossil

A fossil coelacanth discovered by the author in Brazil. It is about 110 million years old and was named in honor of the author as Axelrodichthys.

We are able to guesstimate that the first fishes appeared on Earth about 500 million years ago. This figure is based upon the fossil record. (The author has been an avid collector of fish fossils for 40 years. His collection of some 50,000 fossil fishes is to be found at the American Museum of Natural History in New York City.) Before that, life was probably present for another half billion years in the waters of the world which, surprisingly enough, were probably divided between fresh and salt. But our first accurate records are only available from

record; lots of fossil sharks are known . . . only from their teeth. It is interesting that as I dug koi pools in Florida near Bradenton I found thousands of fossil shark teeth in the sand. No sign of any other part of the shark, mind you, only the teeth!

This book could easily be filled with the history of fishes from their first fossil record to today, but since everything once lived in the water, our evolution traces back to spineless (animals without backbones) things that lived in the water . . . to animals with backbones (vertebrates) that

15

lived in the water . . . to fishes. Something to think about is that unborn human children are aquatic vertebrates, just like fishes! The first fishes probably had no bones in their skeletons but, like present day sharks, skates, and rays, had cartilaginous skeletons. (Actually, the ancestors of sharks, skates, and rays probably had bony skeletons but lost them in the course of evolution.)

Where Does the Koi Fit In?
One of the largest families of fishes is the family Cyprinidae.

carp). The Chinese were the first to breed goldfish (*Carassius auratus*) and koi (*Cyprinus carpio*), and their aquaria dated back to the 1300's. Japanese colored carp only date back to 1800 or so, when according to legend the first carp with a red spot on the head was hatched. Koi, like goldfish, barbs, rasboras, labeos, danios, and bitterlings, are all related. In most cases they are hardy and make excellent aquarium pets. The warm-water species are, naturally, a lot more delicate than the cold water species.

Comet goldfish look almost like small koi except for their shorter dorsal fin base and more forked tail. Goldfish and koi are closely related and may be kept together in the same pond.

This family contains freshwater fishes from Africa, Eurasia, and North America, with none native to South America and Australia (although today cyprinids are everywhere in the form of introductions of goldfish and

Now that you know all about koi, it might be well to consider having them as pets. Assuming that you are an intelligent, dependable conserver of animal life, the koi in your possession are most likely to keep growing until they outgrow your container. This is true of large outdoor ponds, pools, or ditches . . . and aquaria, too. Koi, as a rule, can grow to almost 2 feet in length. Certainly 18 inches is a usual size for a grown koi that has been cared for properly. In an aquarium they are usually stunted unless their tank

Long-finned koi are a reality, even though this is a very stylized drawing.

is large and the water is constantly moving to remove their waste materials and give them the oxygen they require.

So, if you start with koi, your first problem is success. What do you do with 18-inch carp? Well, to be heartless about it, you can eat them. That's what the Japanese do. I can never forget the first time I visited the Yoshida Koi Farm in Japan. They ceremoniously brought before me a magnificent koi with fabulous coloring. The fish would easily have fetched a month's pay at auction. They quickly cut off the fish's head, scaled the body, and removed the entrails. Then they sliced the body into thin, mouth-sized wafers and served it on a beautifully garnished platter. Though I had to eat it because of my responsibilities of courtesy, it was very difficult. Since then I have become a carp aficionado, and every time I visit eastern Europe and Russia (four or five times a year), I always eat fresh or pickled carp or "gefilte fish," carp that is ground up with bread crumbs, onions, eggs, and perhaps other fishes and made into fish balls that are boiled. The resulting juice jells as it gets cold in the refrigerator. Eaten with horseradish, it is a tempting delicacy and one of which I am extremely fond. (Forgive me, please!)

Where Does the Koi Fit In?

My Japanese friends tell me that the latest rage in Japan is to have Christmas parties centering around koi. (My first question was why are the Japanese, a Shinto or Buddhist people, celebrating Christmas? I guess that it is probably as good an excuse for a social gathering—which the Japanese love so much—as any and fits in well with their tendency to adopt modified Western behavior.) The family throwing the party buy the biggest and most beautiful koi they can afford, bring it home, and let it live it up for a few days in the bathtub, meanwhile feeding it all types of tidbits. When it comes time to kill the fish and serve it for the party, the animal has become something of a pet and everyone hates to kill it. At the last moment the head of the family wraps it in plastic and puts it in the freezer long enough so it is dead but still perfectly fresh and fine for eating. This whole story sounds a lot like the legend of the Thanksgiving turkey that no one has the heart to kill for dinner, instead keeping it as a pet until next spring. So far as I know, the idea of a Thanksgiving or Christmas koi dinner hasn't been tried here, but you might keep it in mind for that really big specimen that lost all its bright colors last fall.

You must face the problem of what to do with large koi because you will undoubtedly put lots of small koi into your aquarium or pond, and what do you do with them when they grow up? If you won't eat them, then make arrangements for someone to buy them for their own pond or ask your petshop operator to buy them from you. He'll probably be very happy to do so in the spring or late winter, but don't ask him in the fall!

These long-finned koi represent the latest in the breeders' art. After the finnage is stabilized, it will be possible to introduce all the colors koi are noted for, resulting in truly fantastic fish with both flowing fins and gorgeous colors.

Judging Koi

Beauty Lies in the Eyes of the Beholder

For the uninitiated, what makes one koi worth thousands while a very similar looking fish is worth merely a pittance? Basically it's merely a matter of perceived beauty. The Japanese have a series of standards for judging koi. In the 1950's when I visited many koi shows, standards were predicated on an ideal koi. Unfortunately, the ideal koi never existed, so arbitrarily the judging was based upon a 100-point

Judges evaluating entries in a Japanese koi competition.

system under which the body shape of the fish was awarded up to 50 points, the color pattern was awarded up to 20 points, and the color was valued at 30 points. Each fish entered in the contest started out with 100 points and every defect in each category was judged to be worth a penalty of points to be subtracted from the

total value. The fish that ended up with the least number of serious defects won the contest. During the 1980's this basis of fish competitions was changed to giving points for special characteristics, making it possible for a fish with outstanding color, for example, to win a contest even though it had serious flaws in size or pattern. Each judge has his (the only judges I ever saw or heard of were men!) own scale of judgment. Many judges now add points for beauty they perceive. Even the way a fish swims or how it carries its fins may impress a particular judge, and he will overlook defects because these special features are more important to him than minor defects.

Fins

Until recently, when long-finned koi appeared on the market, the relative size of a koi's fins was judged. The main fins that were judged were the pectoral fins, because these fins are the most visible when the fish is viewed from above. The larger the pectorals compared to the size of the body, the more beautiful the fish appeared to the judge. On the other hand, if the pectorals were dwarfed, misshapen, improperly colored, or not identical in size, the fish would almost always be disqualified.

Deformations of the dorsal and tail fins also resulted in disqualification, but since the long-finned varieties have come onto the scene, the more deformed the fins are, the more valuable the fish.

It is very interesting that this change is developing, because the very word "koi" is not a Japanese word. It is of Chinese origin and was the name given to the fish by the Chinese. Japanese officially call the koi "Nishikigoi."

Body Shape

The Japanese recognize four basic body shapes when the fish is viewed from the side: the Shinshu; the wild, elongated koi that has escaped from a pond and has returned via generations of inbreeding to a natural form that swims very well and has colors that blend in with the pond in which it lives; the Ishugrudei; and the Nippon or Japanese strain.

In cross-section, there are ideals for a theoretical slice through the mid-section of the fish, with the slice starting in front of the dorsal fin and proceeding through the pelvic fins. The ideal is a perfect circle, and though a koi has never achieved the ideal, there are many koi that are rounded in cross-section rather than being oval.

The Japanese consider body shape to be most important and usually allot 50 points for the various categories considered under body shape. There are usually five specific tests of body shape. These are depth to length ratio; finnage; head shape; straight line from the center of the snout to the center of the top of the tail; and the side profile.

Depth to Length Ratio A characteristic of every species of fish in nature is the ratio of its height to its length. In cultured fish such as the koi this characteristic is inbred for the

This magnificent koi is a Kin Matsuba or "gold pine needle" colored carp.

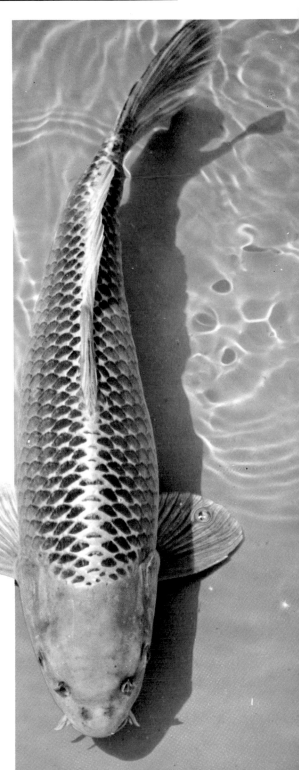

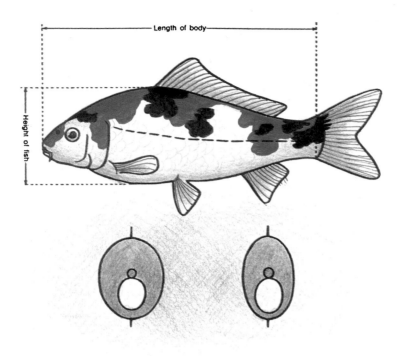

Length of body

Height of fish

The ideal koi's body dimensions are calculated by the number of times the height or depth of the body fits into the length. Typical good koi are 2½-3 times as long as they are deep.

Ideally, the Japanese would like to breed koi that have a perfectly circular cross-section at the deepest part of their body height. Body shape is a very important consideration for the judges.

ideal. Excellent koi specimens have a depth to length ratio of between 1:2.5 and 1:3.

Finnage Paired fins must be the same on both sides of the fish. The single fins, dorsal and caudal, must be well formed. Fish with deformed finnage due to genetic defects, wounds, or disease are usually disqualified. In most cases a standard has evolved where certain varieties, like the red and white Kohaku, must have pure white pectorals.

Head Shape In the head are the lips, jaws, gill covers, eyes, and the general bulk of the head itself. If any one of the parts of the head is deformed, the fish is usually disqualified. Many breeders argue that it is only a matter of time before koi are bred into the identical varieties as goldfish. Therefore growths about the eyes (water bubble-eyes), growths on the head (lionheads), or even upturned or bulging eyes (celestials) may never be developed if these characteristics

22

are ignored. The same is true of nasal bouquets and other head anomalies. Thus far the Japanese have rigorously rejected this type of breeding direction, but as more and more Westerners begin breeding koi in large quantities, these mutant forms are likely to appear and perhaps breeders will fix these grotesque characteristics into a goldfish-like koi.

Center Line When viewed from above, the ideal koi must have an absolutely straight line from the tip of the snout to the tail, including the tail fin itself. The fish must also be bilaterally symmetrical; thus, if the fish were cut along this line both sides would be the same. Any curvature of the spine would be an immediate disqualification. Naturally, a pregnant female swollen with eggs would be excused from disqualification on this basis.

Side Profile The Japanese recognize the four profiles mentioned earlier. These profiles must be balanced with the fins, though almost all koi are basically the same in general side profile. According to the judges, the profile of the fish affects the way it swims and thus profile is important.

Colors of the Koi
Here we have a true discrepancy between Oriental tastes and Western ideals. To most Westerners, the more vivid and intense the color of the fish the better it is. The Japanese look for purity of color rather than intensity. If a fish is white and red, then the red must be uniform . . . it doesn't matter how deep the red is as long as it's only one shade of red. The white must be pure white. The edges where the red and white meet must be sharply defined and uniform in color. Take a vividly red and white

The four body types recognized by Japanese judges are: A) the Shinshu, which has a round head and is not very attractive in body form; B) and C) are wild forms that either degenerated from koi that escaped into the natural water system or are the basic European types; and D) the ideal Japanese body style.

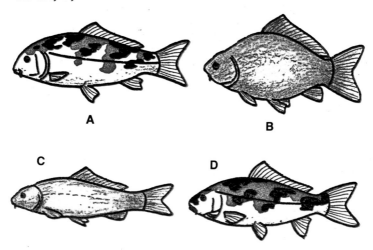

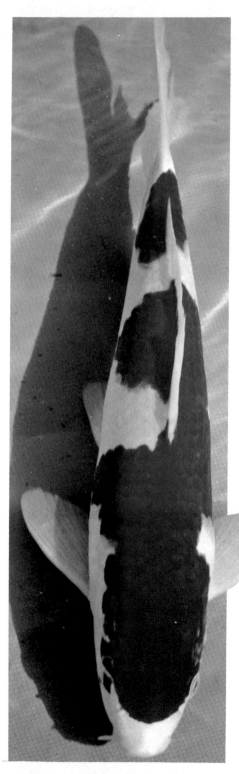

fish. If within the patch or patches of red there is a single white spot, then the fish is not a good specimen. The same is true of the white areas. If there is a single red scale, the fish is penalized.

The Pattern

Most of you have heard of the Rorschach test. Dr. Rorschach was a Swiss psychiatrist who died in 1922. He discovered that he could learn quite a bit from people who suggested to him their interpretations of a series of ink blotches of different designs. He wrote a book about the different personalities and how they reacted to different kinds of blotches. The same type of thing probably is true of some modern paintings where people see what they want to see. Unfortunately, or perhaps fortunately, the same also is true of koi. Koi do not breed true as yet. Like guppies, where every wild guppy is different from every other wild guppy (males only!), koi do not breed very true to their own parents' colors or patterns. Thus

The Kohaku is a very popular and well developed pattern in koi since it has been selectively inbred for many years. A Kohaku is two-colored. One of my Japanese friends "read" this pattern as a French poodle viewed from above.

each judge will have his own idea of which pattern is more or less interesting . . . *providing the colors fall within certain acceptable patterns.*

The Japanese talk about balance. They insist on some

colorless portions on either the mouth or the tail. A solidly colored fish has no appeal unless it is a metallic color. The color of the pattern is only important as long as it is pure. The patterns have names. A fish with three distinct blotches on its body (when viewed from above) might appear like the stepping-stones that are so popular in Japanese gardens, thus there is a "stepping-stone" pattern. By looking at some of the photos of champion fish in this book, you can better understand the kinds of patterns that appeal to the Japanese. You are, of course, entitled to your own opinions, too.

General Quality

Somehow Japanese koi judges can look at a fish and immediately fall in love with it. This happens between people, and it probably happens between young boys and cars, rich people and works of art, etc. It is best captured by the feeling "I've got to have this for my own."

Certainly a high quality pertains to ALL the individual characteristics. While one fish

This magnificent Hi-Utsuri is 20 inches long and has a very interesting color pattern when viewed from above. The colors are intense as well, making this a champion quality fish.

might have better color or a better pattern, another fish might have a better COMBINATION of characteristics without excelling in any one characteristic. This what is meant by general quality.

Under this heading the Japanese also speak about beauty and elegance . . . daintiness . . . gracefulness when it swims. These are also considerations when general quality is under review. Though general quality only receives 10 points by most judges' tally sheets, it's quality that costs the most. High quality fish sell for thousands!

Size

The Japanese are a diminutive race much smaller in physical size than most Westerners. Some geneticists consider this a defect in inbreeding . . . "No hybrid vigor" they say. Americans, Canadians, Australians, and Scandinavians, most of whom are mixtures of many inbred generations, are much taller on average.

For this reason the Japanese place rather special values on size. Just imagine a Sumo wrestler. To most Westerners he is rather grotesque, but to some Japanese he is idolized.

This Aigoromo is basically a Kohaku (two-colored red and white) crossed with an Asagi. This is an excellent quality fish. The light blue tinges in the red pattern are caused by dark pigment under transparent scales.

So too is the large koi. In every fish competition I witnessed in Japan, the larger koi always won out over competitors with almost equal or even slightly better colors and patterns. This means that mostly female koi win contests, for though young males grow faster than young females, in the long run older females are much larger than older males.

In all cases, however, the fish must be well balanced and muscular . . . just like a weight-lifting champion versus a beer-drinking man of the same weight.

This lovely Shiro Bekko has a very interesting two color pattern. Some koi lovers appreciate the isolated patches of color (sometimes called "stepping stones"), but this particular fish has too many such patches for them to be considered as stepping stones. This Shiro Bekko, though, has a very interesting pattern of color. Its black is intense and the white is pure. The fish is about two feet long.

Competitions

If you want to join a koi club you must make that contact through the aquarium shop through which you purchased your koi and its food. Unfortunately, the clubs that the author has been tracking are anything but permanent, and like most clubs, they revolve around one or two people who keep it going. But you should visit other koi lovers in your neighborhood, and, should you be lucky enough to make a foreign trip (especially to Japan), you might want to contact others who have the same hobby but are in another country. I have made lots of new friends that way.

Competitions The rallying point of any koi club is the annual competition. Not only is this vital for maintaining interest in the club by its members, but it is the major fundraiser, it brings local dealers closer to the group (perhaps even

A koi show in Japan will attract thousands of visitors, each of whom pays an admission charge. The entrants also pay an admission charge, and this money (minus expenses) is given as prize money. Japanese koi clubs support themselves with this income.

offering special deals on fish), and, most importantly, it attracts new koi lovers to the club. By inviting school children and allowing outsiders to see the fish (for a fee, of course), you have an opportunity to spread the hobby of koi-keeping.

The basis of any competition is the point values by which the koi are judged. If your competition is a minor one with only amateur koi hobbyists, then you want a point system where size, for example, does not play an important part. Perhaps for such competitions you might want to award a special "collections" prize to the hobbyist who has more different varieties of a higher class than anyone else. Only the particular structure of your own club should dictate point values.

The Judge Koi judges are hard to find unless you find them in Japan or Hawaii, where koi are most popular. In any case, the petshop owner who sold you your koi should be able to give you some leads on finding a koi judge. You should NOT try to have one of your club members judge his fellow hobbyists. This causes unnecessary friction in your club. Find someone from another club

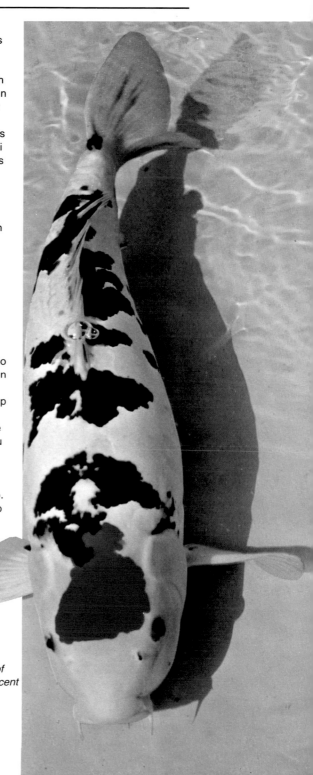

This Tancho Sanshoku is a three-colored koi with a red head patch. The head patch can only be red and must be the only red on the fish. The fact that this Tancho Sanshoku has red eye rims means that it is completely defective for this type of fish, but otherwise it is a magnificent specimen.

if you can. If it's a truly great event with outside revenues from admission fees generated by inviting the public, then perhaps you can get a more qualified person.

Remember: Ask the judge for the basis of his judgment point system.

Point Systems There are as many possibilities of point systems as there are points of view. Presented below are two point systems that have been used successfully.

OLD STYLE JAPANESE SYSTEM
Body Shape .... 50 pts
   Depth to Length Ratio . 10 pts
   Finnage......................... 10 pts
   Head Shape .... 10 pts
   Center Line................... 10 pts
   Side Profile................... 10 pts
   In this category any deformation of any of these characteristics will result in a disqualified fish.
Color Pattern....................... 20 pts
   This is a Rorschach test situation where "beauty lies in the eyes of the beholder." That's why you need an experienced judge.

This very interesting koi is called a Kaga Showa. This variety falls within the three-colored Showa, the Showa Sanshoku. It is basically a red- and white-scaled fish with a coating of gray scales. The head spot is very interesting, and the pattern reminds one of the pine needle design.

Basically, the color pattern should be interesting. Distinct areas should be separated by a contrasting color. In the case of solid color fish, the purity of shade is judged. In mixed color fish, then the mixture must set an interesting pattern. It is difficult to separate the category of color from color pattern.

Color .... 30 pts

Any color is acceptable in a koi, but some are rarer than others. The blue family of colors, including purple, green, and blue-black, is almost never seen as solid patches except on those fish such as the Bekko, where the black is intense and not well marked with blue. There are instances in Bekkos where a clear scale overlaps a black scale, this very small area appearing blue when compared to the surrounding scales.

Intensity .... 10 pts
Purity .... 10 pts
Well-marked edges ...... 10 pts

MODERN JAPANESE SYSTEM

Mr. Takeo Kuroki, the author of a very fine book on koi that suffers only because he uses strictly Japanese terms and

This magnificent Aka Matsuba, the red pine needle koi, is a Matsuba group color variation. Basically it is a red fish, and the scalation must present the effect of looking like a pine cone. It doesn't take too much imagination to see why this variety is referred to as a "pine" something, but "pine cone" might be better than "pine needle." This fish is not brilliantly colored; the red should be much more intense and bright.

doesn't explain their meanings, has proposed a point system that better fits the current Japanese scene. His system is based upon the Old Style Japanese System, the so-called "traditional system," and differs only in point values. His suggestion is:

Body Shape .... 30 pts

In Mr. Kuroki's book he refers to body shape as "figure." He doesn't mean the "figure" that is variable with feeding, but the genetic "figure" that includes over- or under-feeding but basically is the shape of the fish.

Color .... 20 pts

Pattern .... 20 pts

Quality .... 10 pts

Elegance .... 10 pts

This basically refers to the fish as an entire animal. How well the color lies on the fish; how the pattern fits in; how it swims; etc.

Imposing Appearance .... 10 pts

By this Mr. Kuroki means the size of the fish. Not that size

This Kin Ki-Utsuri is a basically "reflection" or mirror-like metallic koi with a beautiful golden reflection. The more recent standards for this fish has been revised to call for an unblemished solid red head. Yet when Tozo Takahashi produced this fish in his koi farm in Yamakoshi Village, Niigata Prefecture in Japan, it was a sensation. Unfortunately Takahashi-san never perfected the strain.

alone matters, but it is quite well known that many strains of koi lose their color as they get older (getting older means getting larger). Thus a large colorless fish is sold by the pound, while a large fish with championship qualities could be worth a fortune.

While it would be wonderful to recommend the adoption of Mr. Kuroki's point system for the Western world, it just wouldn't work because the "Imposing Appearance" could well be decided by someone's ability to dedicate a large pool with lots of natural food to just a few fish. This would almost guarantee a large fish or two in a dozen years.

No, it won't be simple. Each committee must construct their own point system based upon their particular area and the type and quality of fish that they expect to have compete. If some special fish is shown that skews the entire point system, merely give it a special award and judge the other fish on the premeditated standard.

By the way—the terms "fish" and "fishes" might require some explanation. If you have two or more koi, you have two or more fish; if you have one koi and one goldfish, you have two fishes. The term fish becomes plural only when referring to two or more different species. Thus, the fishes in the ocean are colorful, but koi are fish that also are colorful.

This Hi Kage Utsuri is basically a red fish with reflecting, metallic scales. There is a black marking pattern, but overall the scales are covered with a blue or gray cast. This particular specimen is very nice because of the interesting pattern, the magnificent body shape, and nice coloration with some pine needle markings, too.

Breeding Koi

Koi are very easy to breed. As a matter of fact, they can be said to breed by themselves!

Although young males two years old may be used for breeding, females must be at least three years old. If you have the inclination, it is best to separate the koi into males and females and keep them isolated from each other by splitting your formal pond in half or by using two ponds. Males in the three-year class are much slimmer than females of equal age when viewed from above. In the spring, before spawning, females are fatter and distended with eggs.

If you want large quantities of fish you should isolate the female and feed her heavily as soon as she starts eating in the spring. Especially offer her shrimp, clams, and koi pellets many times a day. Put her into the pond in which you expect her to spawn. She will need some spawning medium. Spanish moss has been used for fish spawning for 100 years; use it if you can find it. If not, gather clumps of soft evergreen branches by clipping the soft ends from the spring growth of evergreen trees. Tie them in a clump as large as the pond can hold. Certainly a clump 3 feet in diameter is as large as you would need for each female. You'll need something to weight down the clump, though more often than not the anchors that I use get loose and the clump floats to the surface. I have often seen the fish swim almost out of the water to get atop the clump and spawn. I have never seen active males and plump females ignore each other. They always spawn . . . that's why there are so many of them. It is not unusual to have 400,000 eggs!

The ideal setup is a pond for spawning and raising the young. This can be a plastic tank, either pliable or rigid (even a kiddy pool), in which the female and the spawning medium are placed. Males are selected when they have the tell-tale nuptial tubercles on their pectoral fins. Sometimes the males have these tubercles on other parts of their bodies, too, but they are most obvious on the pectoral fins. Two or three males are placed with a plump female. Breeding usually takes place within 24 hours, usually in the early morning. Once the males are put in with the female, a submersible heater that can slowly bring up the water temperature by 5°F will greatly expedite spawning.

Once the fish have spawned, they should be removed from the spawning pond and the fry should be raised separately from their parents. This will ensure large quantities of babies. Hatching takes up to a week if the water is cold but may be as quick as 72 hours if the water is warm.

If only a few baby koi are desired, you can probably leave the adults to their own devices in whatever kind of pond setup you have. They will spawn in the spring and a few babies will survive if they have some places to hide after the eggs hatch. Provide a dense planting of water lilies or, even better, large clumps of such spawning plants as *Myriophyllum*, *Elodea*, and *Nitella*. The previously described clump of evergreen branches tied together and weighted down will also prove helpful in saving the babies from being mistakenly eaten by their parents, who don't recognize them as fish until they reach an inch or two in length.

As soon as you see spawning activity in the pool, try to find some daphnia or other small crustaceans to feed the developing fry. Since the eggs hatch usually in from four to seven days and it takes another few days to absorb their yolk sacs and begin their first free-swimming stages when they hunt for food, you should make plans to collect, hatch, or buy some live daphnia. Two weeks of feeding daphnia should be enough to carry the young into the powdered dry food stage. Merely crush the floating pellets that you feed the adults and feed both the powder and uncrushed pellets at the same time. You should soon be able to notice little koi darting from hiding place to hiding place. Made brazen by the appearance of food, they might even dash out for a morsel. Even if you don't offer daphnia and your pool is not too immaculately cleaned, you will find that a few babies will survive and grow into adulthood very quickly.

This Ai Showa is an offshoot of the three-colored Showa. It features red scales with blue tinges. Basically there are no blue koi, but when the dark skin pigment formed by melanin or melanophores is covered over by transparent scales, the resulting dilution of the melanin gives a hint of blue or gray. So, like goldfish and roses, a real blue is still a very much sought-after color that continues to elude breeders.

Breeding koi in an aquarium is considered impossible and impractical. Of course it could be done if the tank were large enough, but what would you then do with so many eggs and developing fry? If you only want some koi for your home aqarium, don't have great aspirations of being a koi breeder. Koi really need some drastic (but slow) temperature changes plus complete water changes before they are truly prepared for spawning. These physical requirements are difficult to accomplish in the usual home aquarium. Koi a few inches long are very inexpensive, so it's really a lot cheaper to buy them than to raise just a few. Young koi are basically colorless. They develop colors and patterns as they grow.

Below: The gnomish fisherman set before a rustic footbridge adds a touch of whimsicality to the natural setting employed in this garden pond.

Water cascades from the upper pool at background and flows down to a lower pond after being channeled through the conduit formed of large irregular rocks joined with cement; the variety of plants allowed to proliferate at the sides of the conduit add much to the scene.

37

In one morning of spawning, two males and one female can produce 200,000 to 400,000 eggs as they thrash about among the evergreen spawning medium.

This terraced series of interconnected ponds looks plain but is difficult to construct and maintain; water must be pumped from the lowest ponds back up to the highest, where it is recirculated through the water channel at top.

Closeup views of koi eggs as they are about to hatch (below) and after hatching. Even the eggs that do not adhere to floating vegetation but fall to the bottom hatch.

Koi are available in millions of color patterns and color combinations. Like wild guppies, no two are exactly alike.

Varieties of Koi

Koi are an inbred mutant strain or strains of carp. The scientific name of the fish, *Cyprinus carpio*, also applies to a Eurasian fish that is a common foodfish throughout the eastern European countries. It is sold alive in most cases and considered a delicacy eaten only on special holidays because it is so expensive. Having been introduced into temperate waters all over the world, carp are internationally known and eaten.

What we Westerners call "German carp" or "mirror carp" (with a few enlarged scales) the Japanese call "Doitsugoi." "Doitsu" is the Japanese phonetic equivalent of "Deutsche," an adjectival form of the German word meaning "Germanic." The "goi" is the Japanese equivalent of the Chinese "koi." There are four basic body shapes of koi, but this book is mainly concerned with what the Japanese call "Nishikigoi." This term is an

White Doitsugoi (German mirror carp). The top fish was crossed with an Asagi to produce a red-bellied koi (bottom) called Shusui or "autumn sky." This fish was developed by a Japanese goldfish breeder named Kichigoro Akiyama at the turn of the century (1900).

This Gin Sui (Silver Shusui) is another magnificent "autumn sky" variety, while the fish below is a Goshiki Shusui whose red belly is barely distinguishable in this photo.

The author's favorites are these metallic golden German koi called "Koshi no Hisoka" or "Etsu no Hisoka." They actually look like they were painted in metallic gold.

invented word that is applied to koi that are bred for color and color pattern. There are now many different classes or groups depending upon their color, color pattern, scalation, and finnage. While long-finned koi are now a reality, they still have not been bred in every color and pattern. Breeders are still working on improving the finnage. Once that genetic characteristic is fixed, they will probably improve the color and pattern characteristics.

The Kohaku A koi whose basic color is white adorned with distinct red patches is called a "Kohaku." Because red and white is the favorite color combination of the Japanese and is reminiscent of their flag, the Japanese are very partial to this color. The best examples of Kohaku almost always win Best in Show. Since the color patterns in Kohaku apply equally well to other basic colors, we will look into those colors and color patterns carefully.

The typical white koi with red patches is the Kohaku. Some people call it the "Nippon" because red and white are the main colors of the Japanese flag. It is the overall favorite color of the many colors in which koi are bred.

Varieties of Koi

The STEPPING-STONE or STEP TYPE pattern is based upon the typical Japanese garden where stones are laid down for people to walk upon since no Japanese garden is paved with asphalt, tar, or cement! Even koi ponds rarely have bridges, but many have steps extending upward from the water, enabling a visitor to walk onto the pond and observe the fish swimming at their feet. The stepping-stone pattern is merely a set of red blotches that are distinct from each other and in a single straight line. Thus a pattern where two red blotches are side by side, even though the rest are in the right order, eliminates the fish from being a stepping-stone pattern. The edges of the red steps must be clear and sharply defined. The quality of the fish is basically judged by the number of steps and their equality of size. Thus there are two-step, three-step, and four-step Kohakus.

The GOTENZAKURA is the Sakura (cherry blossom) koi. "Goten" applies to a royal residence, castle, or palace. Thus this pattern is very highly considered. It is merely a disqualified Stepping-stone in which the steps are not in a straight line, are scattered, and may have either a balanced pattern or a random pattern. They must be bilaterally symmetrical, thus for each red blotch on one side of the imaginary line from the snout to the base of the caudal fin there must be a corresponding blotch on the other side.

The Gotenzakura or "palace cherry blossom koi." It is a Kohaku of impure quality since the red patches have irregular instead of smooth edges.

Kohaku that have isolated red patches or "steps" astride the back are named according to the number of steps. The fish at the top is a Nidan Kohaku (Two-Step); the fish below is a Sandan (Three-Step) Kohaku.

45

The KINZAKURA is a Gotenzakura where the red scales have gold edging. It is one of the most prized of all color varieties.

The PARALLEL HIGH derives its name from what the Japanese call the "Straight Hi." The Hi spot is the red spot. When one long red mark runs along the dorsal edge of the koi it is called a Parallel High. This is a rare but not very interesting fish. More interesting is the Hi Blitz. This curious combination of a German

The golden cherry blossom koi shown above differs from the Gotenzakura by having gold edging to its red scales. It is known as the Kinzakura. "Cherry blossom" is spelled "sakura" or "zakura." The fish below is another famous Kohaku variety known as a Menkaburi. It has a solid red patch covering its whole head.

Two other red koi are noteworthy, though there are easily another dozen red koi varieties that are recognized by koi lovers. The upper fish is a Mizuho Ohgon. This is a reddish orange koi with mirror carp scalation. "Mizuho" was what "Nippon" is today, an old term referring to the country. Actually it means the ear of the rice plant, since the dark scales along the back resemble a ripened ear or head of rice. The lower fish is a cherry blossom Ohgon, Sakura Oh-gon. Some people see a pine cone pattern in this fish as well.

word "blitz," which can mean a bolt of lightning, and Hi, which is the red spot, defines a Parallel High whose single long red mark along the dorsal edge takes the shape of an imaginary bolt of red lightning.

The DOITSU KOHAKU NAPOLEON is a figment of Japanese imagination. It is a

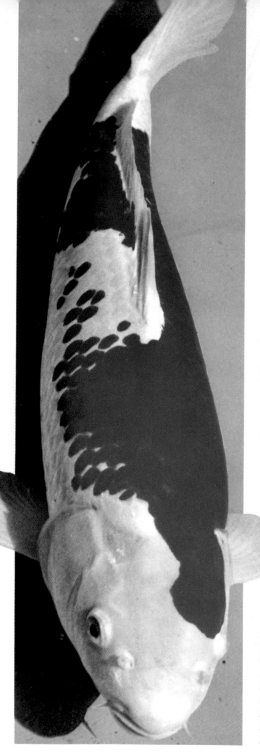

basically blotched red-white pattern in which the Japanese swear to see the familiar hat that Napoleon was reputed to wear and that he made famous. "Beauty lies in the eyes of the beholder" again! For whatever reason, this pattern is only recognized on German carp.

The MOUNT FUJI KOHAKU is a temporary juvenile characteristic. The light colored lumps on the head of some koi remind the Japanese of their famous Fujiyama, Mount Fuji, thus the name for this fish. The lumps rarely remain for more than two or three years.

The SHIROMUJI or plain solid white koi is an extremely popular koi in the West, but it is fed to the birds in Japan since it has no value. The fish is absolutely gorgeous, with its snow-white skin visible through crystal-clear scales.

The AKAMUJI is the opposite of the Shiromuji. Shiro or shirao means white in Japanese, while aka means red. The Akamuji is a

The Fawn Kohaku, Kanoko Kohaku, owes its name to an imaginative koi breeder who thought this looked like young deer adorned with white markings on a tan background. If you look closely, ignoring the red, you can barely discern the light tan background, especially on the head.

Solid-colored koi are not valued. This Red Koi is merely an Akamuji (red koi).

This Shiromuji or white koi is adorned with some remnant mirror carp scales, but it is still almost without admirers in Japan. The metallic adornment makes it a bit more valuable.

A dark red, even an almost black-red, solid colored koi is referred to as a Beni Goi or Beni Koi.

solid red koi. In the West it is very expensive and very popular. In Japan it is a cull. High prices are commanded in the West when the red in the Akamuji is very dark and solid. Then the fish is called a Higoi, Hi pertaining to the red markings and goi meaning koi. Higoi have little value in Japan and are probably one of the most expensive varieties in the West.

These are very beautiful koi. They are known as "Voluptuous Beauties" or "Enyu."

Sometimes the red gets very dark, even tending to be black. Then the Higoi is called a Hiaka or even a Benigoi. When any of these solid red fish has white fins, it is called an Aka-hajiro.

The Tancho Kohaku (top) is recognized by the single round red mark on the head. The tanch is a white crane that has a red head mark. The fish below it is a Tancho Sanshoku Ginrin. The 3-colored koi has rows of ginrin (metallic scales) only along the dorsal edge. The black and white koi is a Shiro Utsuri Ginrin, a "White Reflection" carp with black markings and rows of ginrin. The lower fish is a Ginrin Kohaku (Kohaku Ginrin).

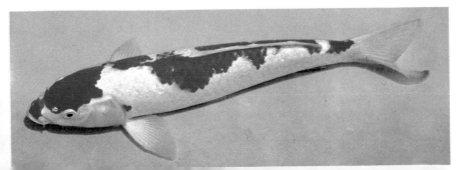

This beautiful koi is called a Showa Sanshoku. The "Showa" means modern since it is the name of the current dynasty. The "Sanshoku" merely means "three-colored," referring to the red, white, and black.

The TANCHO-KOHAKU is a white carp with a beautiful Hi spot on the head only. This mark must not touch the eyes, nose, or mouth. This Tancho koi is sometimes referred to as the "Cherry koi" in the West.

The KANOKO-KOHAKU or KAWARIMONO is a two-colored koi in which the red is dispersed irregularly over the body, with each red scale ideally separated from each other by a white scale. That is the ideal, but in reality any fish with lots of isolated red scales is called a Kanoko.

The Platinum or Silver Kohaku, KIN-FUJI or HIKARIMOYO, is a koi in which the white is metallic and shining, which is a very appealing color to everyone who sees it. Usually this fish is a hybrid of the Ogon (metallic golden) and the Kohaku. Champion Kin-Fuji have no Hi on the head and the red is very bright and distinct.

Color Patterns Other Than Red and White

There are as many color patterns and colors as one imagination can describe. Rather than invent even more colors, the following patterns are recognized by most Japanese koi show committees.

The TAISHO-SANKE is a three (San) colored koi. Basically it is a Kohaku with black. The black markings are called "Sumi" marks; the red are called "Hi" marks. A good Sanke shouldn't have any black on its head and should basically be an excellent Kohaku with good black markings. Black fin rays in the pectorals are appreciated, especially three stripes only. The Taisho-Sanke appears in all the other variations as the Kohaku. Thus, for example, an Aka-Sanke is a three colored koi that is all red with a pattern of one or more black markings.

Add reflecting scales along the side to this Taisho Sanshoku (above) and you have a Taisho Sanshoku Ginrin. By adding mirror carp scales to the fish below, the Japanese have produced a Doitsu Taisho Sanshoku.

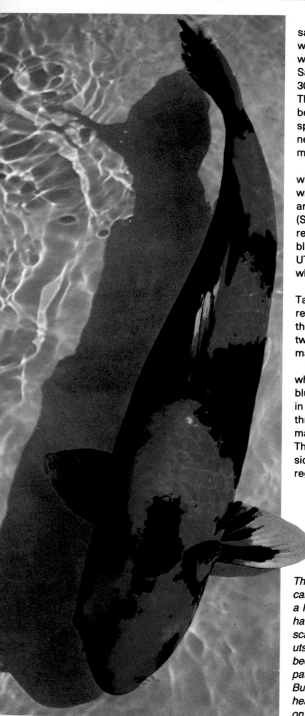

The SHOWA-SANSHOKU is the same as the Taisho-Sanke except where the skin of the Taisho is white, the skin of the Showa-Sanshoku is black. Not more than 30% of white scales is elegant. The bases of the pectorals must be solid black. This variety has special standards about the necessity for having a well marked Hi on its head.

The UTSURI is a koi group in which the scales are reticulated with cone-shaped markings that are very subdued. The White (Shiro) Utsuri has white reticulations on black skin. It has black pectoral fin bases. The KI-UTSURI is the same except the white is replaced with yellow.

The BEKKO derives from the Taisho-Sanke and has skin that is red, white, or yellow. On top of the skin is black. Thus this is a two colored fish with black markings on red, white, or yellow.

The ASAGI is a koi pattern in which the back is blue. Not a true blue, for this doesn't really exist in koi, but a blackish scale through which the white skin may make it appear light or dark blue. This fish must have red on the sides of the face, in the belly region, and on the bases of the

This beautiful two-colored red carp with black markings is called a Hi Utsuri. The Utsuri group have very subtly reticulated scales. "Hi Utsuri" means "red utsuri." It is a very popular fish because of the interesting patterns. Can you see the Butterfly Fish markings on the head? How about the flying witch on the shadow side of the fish?

The fish above is a Gin Utsuri. This is a basically white Utsuri (Shiro Utsuri) with an Ohgon metallic sheen. The Kin Ki Utsuri shown below is the "golden yellow reflection koi" with a much deeper golden yellow than the Gin Utsuri. This strain was developed in 1959 by Takahashi-san.

fins. The scales must have a reticulated pattern with a light reticulation and a darker inside.

The SHUSUI is an Asagi pattern on a German (Doitsu) carp. The back becomes very dark and the reticulation is very marked in this strain.

Cross an Asagi and a Kohaku and you get a KOROMO. This word probably derives from the English "chrome." It is a koi with a basic two color Kohaku pattern and lots of blue, reticulated scales, and mottled black markings all over the fish. There are some weird-looking koi in this group. I once saw a pure white koi, Shiromuji, with 25 solid black scales over which there was a red reticulation. It was memorable.

A very interesting group of Nishikigoi are the truly colored carps called collectively KAWARIMONO. There is no single fish that is a Kawari, but rather each has its own classification. Thus a very dark, but not black, fish is a Karasu. Karasu means dark, thus a Karasugoi is a dark koi. Ki means yellow, thus a Kigoi is a yellow koi. Midori, a favorite Japanese name for a business or a girl, means green, thus a Midorigoi is

scalation. When these OHGON or metallic koi are imperfect they are called Kinginrin. The Kinginrin were the first metallics, thus they were revered and tolerated. As the strain was perfected and solid metallics became available, the Japanese refused to discard their defective metallics, and thus they preserved the Kinginrin category.

Another official group that crosses other lines is the fish with a perfectly round Hi (red) mark on its head. It can be any other variety, even pure white Shiromuji, but if the Hi mark is truly elegant then the fish can be a super champion.

These are the basic color patterns to be found in koi. Of

This crude monotone koi is called a Silver bum (hobo) or Gin Bo.

a green koi. The Matsuba is the pine needle koi. The Japanese go on and on in describing colors that don't quite fit into any other category. Thus the Kawarimono are attractive kois that don't develop true patterns, yet their lack of a distinct pattern is itself a recognizable trait.

The author's favorite group is the metallics, referred to by the Japanese as the OHGONS. The OHGON is basically a metallic gold koi, but as time developed this metallic gold koi also appeared in platinum, orange, red, and deep gold (Yamabuki), plus these same colors in the

course crosses made between these basic varieties produce other basic varieties, and the story can go on and on as the Japanese invent new names for these varieties. Perhaps koi have more color and pattern varieties than any other fish or animal. They even have more varieties than guppies! Guppies already exist in nature with varied colors, but the koi exists in nature only as a commonly colored *Cyprinus carpio.*

Thus the world of koi-lovers owes a deep debt of gratitude to the Japanese for their tireless dedication to producing koi.

A Sho Chiku Bai or Pine Bamboo Plum.

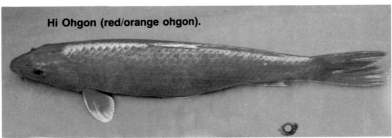

Hi Ohgon (red/orange ohgon).

This Platinum Kohaku, Kin Fuji, or Hikarimoyo has shining white metallic scales. Good Kin Fuji have no hi spot on the head. The red should be very intense. This is a poorly marked specimen.

Koi as Pets

Why Koi Make Such Great Pets

1. Koi are very hardy.
2. Koi do not fight, either among themselves or with other fishes.
3. Koi do not eat other fishes unless they are small fry and are more or less accidentally ingested.
4. Koi grow quickly. Under proper conditions they may grow 8 inches per year; minimally, they grow 4 inches per year.
5. Koi live a long time. Under good care a koi can easily live 50 years, and in Japan 70-year-old koi are not unusual. One reporter claims that Mr. Komei Koshihara owns a female koi 226 years old. She weighs about 20 pounds and is 2½ feet long. Her age was supposedly verified by counting the annual rings in her scales.
6. Koi become tame. They quickly learn to come to the corner of the tank or pool to be fed. They take food from your hand readily after a few weeks of acquaintanceship. In Japan, most koi breeders feed their koi from their own mouths. This "kissing feast," as one Japanese gentleman refers to it, proves the great attraction the koi and their owners develop. It's a good thing koi don't have teeth in their outer jaws . . . merely crushing teeth (pharyngeal teeth) deep in their throats.
7. Koi are good to eat. They are served at all high-class Japanese celebrations when they are available. Japanese refer to them as warrior fish (Samurai) because they do not wriggle and jump when they are cut into slices. The Japanese eat them raw, usually within minutes of their being ritually slaughtered.
8. Koi are indoor-outdoor pets. Children can easily keep koi in a simple aquarium without a heater. Adults can keep them in ponds where they thrive between 40-85°F. They can go without food for a week or two, though this is not a good practice.
9. Koi eat every kind of food that a human can eat, but it's a lot cheaper to buy them floating pellets made especially for koi. They can swallow the pellets quickly and thus the bottom of the tank or pool is not covered with uneaten particles. Also, floating pellets measure the amount of food the koi need. Once they stop eating you just don't feed them any more. Since koi have no stomach as we know it, they eat small quantities at a time. Usually two feedings a day are best, one in the early morning and one after you have your own lunch.
10. Koi are easy to move around. You can keep them in a tank and move them outdoors in the spring, or *vice versa*, depending upon the temperature. They thrive under most conditions though the changes in temperature must be made slowly or they will secrete a mucous coating from their bodies that looks like their skin is coming off.
11. Koi are colorful and restful to watch. The Japanese are a very contemplative people. They can sit and stare into a koi pond for hours, solving their problems as they relax. Many Japanese equate a long, hot bath with a long visit to a koi pond.
12. Koi ponds are decorative and instructive.
13. Koi are profitable. They breed very easily in the spring. Just give them a spawning medium like Spanish moss or a clump of fine roots and you'll have 200,000-400,000 eggs per spawning. Of course you have to have plenty of room for the growing fry and separate them from larger fish until they are an inch or two long.

Things to buy at your pet shop for the koi aquarium: A) large rocks, depending upon the size of the tank; B) crushed gravel for the bottom; C) live daphnia that will clear up the water and then be eaten by the koi; D) a decorative log (most are ceramic ornaments, which are safer than wood); E) a large net; F) some hardy, large plants for decoration.

14. Koi are interesting and photogenic. Just take some of your colorful koi out of your pond and place them in a small children's wading pool (one with a blue bottom is the usual type). Then just photograph them according to the poses you see in this book. They also make great conversation pieces and your children can write great papers for their school work based upon the history and their experiences with their koi. (They'd better leave out the part about eating them!)

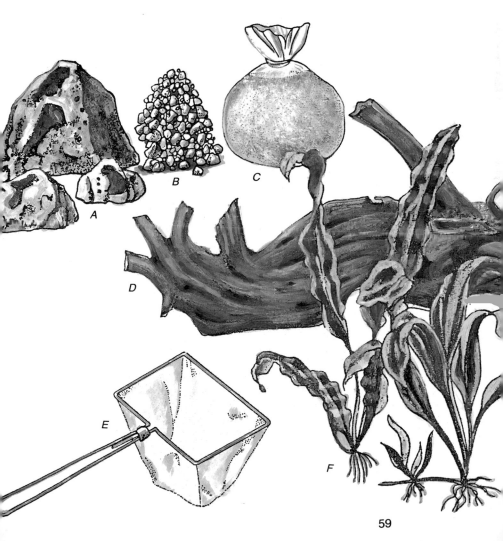

The Aquarium for Koi

Like most pets, the koi must be "caged." For fishes there are two kinds of "cages," either an aquarium or a pond. There is absolutely no valid reason that one cannot keep a koi in an aquarium. In small tanks you can keep small koi; in large tanks large koi. The only question is how small and how large?

The author keeps koi in both his aquaria and his outdoor pond. Just to keep the record straight,

In the center of Moscow, USSR, in the International Hotel, they have several ponds that are laden with gorgeously colored koi swimming in crystal-clear water. You can have the same. Your pet shop will have a plastic pool that you can equip with large slate stones, overhanging plants in their terrestrial flowerpots, and a spray pump.

let's call anything dug into the ground a pond, while anything else is an aquarium . . . even if it's a kiddy pool made of inflated plastic. The aquarium formula for koi depends upon the usual aquarium factors of aeration, filtration, and water temperature. By all means consult an aquarium book for the details of managing an aquarium. An aquarium is as simple to manage as a pond . . . perhaps even simpler, and it has many advantages . . . and disadvantages. Basically, koi are fish that are bred to be viewed from above, so koi that are attractive from the side are not highly valued in the koi community. I keep my baby long-finned koi in an aquarium until they outgrow it. I have about ten young fish that I put into the 200-gallon aquarium when they are 4 inches long. I do not need a heater, pump, or filter, but I use all of them anyway. As the fish get larger, say around 6 inches, I need the filter to keep the water clear because of their droppings and also because the fish's constant searching of the bottom stirs up "dust." A heater only makes them grow faster. They do not need heat as long as the aquarium temperature doesn't drop more than 5° every few hours and never freezes, for then the aquarium might burst! As the fish grow, I can judge the long-fins better and separate the fish I want to sell from the fish I want to breed.

I have pleasure with my koi all year 'round. There are four tanks in my office. At home I have my outside pool, which freezes over for only a month or two, but once the water gets cold I don't see the fish from about mid-November, when they stop eating, until late March or early April. They seem to stop eating when the water

Pet shops that specialize in fishes, especially coldwater fishes like koi and goldfish, also have aeration and filtration equipment. The pumps shown above have air filters that remove the larger dirt particles before pumping the air into the koi pond. The air must be broken into small bubbles with an air stone or other bubble releaser. Shown below are water pumps that are submerged in the pool and blow the water into the air, as shown on the facing page. The height of the neck of the pump is adjustable. These pumps are also used in outside ponds to aerate the water when the pond is over-fertilized and develops an algal bloom. This algal bloom threatens the fish by using up oxygen at night and by using oxygen and producing toxins when they die.

A magnificent informal Japanese koi pond that runs around the house and serves both as a decoration and "fence." Large stepping stones are strategically placed to assist in walking over the pond.

lilies die and start eating again when the lilies sprout, more or less.

You can keep the smaller koi in the outdoor pond until it gets cold and then bring some in for the winter for your aquarium. Then you can put them back out in the springtime, being careful to ensure that the temperatures in the aquarium and the pond are close (within 5°F) before you unceremoniously put them into the pond.

You feed the koi the same thing in an aquarium that you feed them in a pond, except you have to be much more careful in an aquarium that you don't overfeed because smaller bodies of water become polluted from rotting uneaten food faster than do larger bodies of water.

Ponds for Koi The scope of this book does not encompass plans and instructions for building garden pools because of the many factors going into the decision-making process. There are, basically, three kinds of pools for koi keeping on an amateur level. The formal pool is a swimming-pool type of construction that can be as large and deep as you care to build it. It can be decorated with fountains and statues. If I had a swimming pool and stopped swimming, I could easily convert it to a koi pond . . . if my wife would allow it! The informal pool or pond is a body of water that can be a natural pond, a drainage pond, or a hole you dug into the ground, lined with plastic to make it waterproof, and disguised as best you could to make it look like a natural pond. The final variant of koi ponds is the plastic pond made of either collapsible or rigid plastic. Petshops have finally begun to sell plastic pond kits.

Your pet shop will have aeration, filtration, and fountain kits that will assist you in maintaining a clear and healthy koi pond, koi aquarium, or goldfish/ koi pool. Be sure to buy your aeration and filtration equipment locally and ascertain that the dealer will loan you replacement equipment should you develop mechanical problems and have to send the equipment back to the manufacturer for repair or replacement.

The ideal pond is one that is not in the sun, for then you can maintain the water in a crystal-clear condition with a typical large aquarium power filter or a large swimming pool filter equipped with diatomaceous earth filtration. The major problem with outdoor pools is that they become green with algae or so thick with plants that the koi are almost invisible until they come up to feed.

Be careful! Swimming pools are kept sparkling clear with chlorine in heavy concentrations . . . concentrations that would kill koi in a very short time. Even swimming pools turn green from algal blooms when chlorine is not continuously added to the water.

An ideal situation is a constant flow of water from a spring or diverted and filtered water from a nearby running brook. But once you have the idea of what you want, consult someone expert in making pools . . . especially swimming pool builders.

A pool requires an easy way to be emptied, a convenient filtering system, a wall or border height of 12 inches above the level of the water as koi really can . . . and do . . . jump out of the pool, and a cone-shaped bottom so the debris converges in a small area from which it can easily be removed by an aquatic vacuum cleaner or a large (say 6 inches)

63

It is beyond the scope of this book to furnish plans for a koi pond. The simple pond above is made from a plastic liner imbedded in the ground. Complete instructions come with the liner. Pet shops carry several brands of flexible and rigid liners, but usually only in the spring. They can always order one for you while you are digging the hole. The pond below is a more expensive variety. It is made of poured concrete, was designed by an architect, and was executed by professional workmen who installed huge rocks as stepping stones and a foundation.

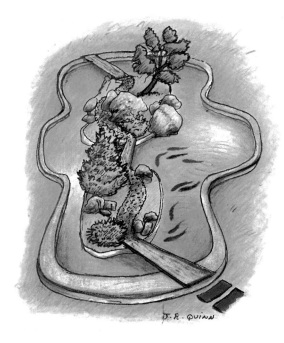

A koi aquarium must have strong plants that are well-rooted and a large open place in the foreground for the fishes to swim freely. Under the gravel a powerful subgravel filter must continually filter the water.

outlet that can drain it when you are changing some of the water. My own pools have water overflow systems in case of heavy rains and clogged up drains. Once or twice a year they overflow anyway, but I have never lost a fish this way. I do lose fish occasionally from their jumping, but koi are so hardy that many times I find them almost dried out, but when I put them back into the water they recuperate. The builder of your pool should know that the deeper the water the easier it is to maintain, but also the clearer it must be for you to see the fish. An ideal depth is 4 to 6 feet. That is, 4 feet deep around the edges closest to the walls and 6 feet in the center where all the mulm accumulates.

There are many kinds of filtration systems, but almost none of them work against the small green algae that produce what is affectionately referred to as "pea soup." The only thing I have used is a constant drip of copper sulfate into the filter, together with a constant slow changing of the water with a water changer that changes the complete pond slowly every two weeks. I use the same water changer principle on my tank and change the water, drop by drop, over the same two-week cycle. Unfortunately, you will have to solve the green water problem yourself, for the particular water you have in your area and the amount of nutrients you put into the pond in the guise of aquarium

A waterfall is created by an underwater submerged pump that pumps the water from the bottom of the pool into a higher pool which overflows into the main pool.
→

Water de-chlorinators are available at pet shops everywhere. If a de-chlorinating preparation is going to be used to treat the water of a garden pond, it makes sense to get the large economy size designed specifically for pond use.

This pool features a picket line of rounded steppingstones arranged in an arc around a central rockpile having a water outflow in its center; natural flagstones set in cement form a stable viewing area.
→

Pet shops carry a number of products that can be used to check the suitability of the water going into the pond as regards its relative acidity/alkalinity values.

food that is uneaten are two of the variables with which you must deal.

I had one system that worked very well for a long time. I split my goldfish pond (in which I also kept koi) into two sections. One section, about 75% of the total surface area and volume of the pond, was dedicated to the fishes; the other section was isolated with screen mesh so the fishes couldn't get in. In this small

→
A wonderful filtering system that can be placed in line with the water pump is shown. The water is passed through four filter chambers filled with activated charcoal and filtering media, as well as a sediment pool. These filters must be made because they are not, as yet, an article of commerce, though some swimming pool filters using diatomaceous earth work wonderfully well.

The overflow pond that feeds the koi pool at the lower level in this illustration is arranged in such a way that its overflow splashes into a secondary overflow pond situated beneath it, thereby agitating and aerating the water before it flows into the main pond. Large rocks border the main pond, but there is a clear area near the island in the main pool. This clear area allows bridging to be placed between the island and the viewing area so that the vegetation on the island can be reached and tended to.

Lying in full sun, this portion of a koi pond will be more subject to the growth of algae and other lower plant forms than those portions of the pond that receive less direct sunlight. Certain of the algal growths can be used as food, but too much is very unsightly.

This drawing shows the basic construction of a formal pond. The subsurface is packed sand about 6" thick, upon which heavier crushed stone is aggregated. Four inches of mesh-reinforced 4,000 p.s.i. concrete is poured atop this floor and a mold can be used to form the sides of 4" steel bar reinforced 3,000 p.s.i. concrete. Then a veneer of brick or stone can be used for decorative value to cover the concrete, or it can be stuccoed. This same pond can be built either completely in the ground or partially extending from the ground, depending upon freezing conditions.

By using an aquarium air pump, most water movement requirements can be solved. Most aquarium pumps are not waterproof, thus they must be housed in a waterproof, vented container or kept in a basement or garage with the plastic airline running to the pool.

section I cultured daphnia and other "water fleas." These small animals thrived on eating algae and they kept the water reasonably free of the "green water" syndrome. I would then daily net out lots of daphnia and feed my tropical fish. Most daphnia only live for a few months, and you have to maintain daphnia eggs from season to season in order to inoculate the pond once again. Daphnia eggs are simple to collect. Merely take a netful of living daphnia and spread them out so they can be sun-dried. Be careful to spread them out or they will rot and be less valuable. When they are dried out, collect them and allow them to dry even more in your garage or basement. Then wait a month and mash them up by squashing the brittle bodies between your palms. This will release the resting eggs from the female daphnias' bodies and they will hatch within a day or two (depending upon temperature) when you drop them into the pool. You can actually sift out the eggs and store them alone, but the additional work is unnecessary.

When setting up your pool for the first time, you should introduce living daphnia. In a white dish they look red. The larger wrigglers are mosquito larvae. You can collect your own living foods from nearby natural ponds, or your pet shop might have some. By crushing freeze-dried daphnia into the pond, the dried eggs will probably hatch, but the fish will instantly eat them.

A cross-section of a circular pond which uses only a bed 12" thick of crushed stone covered with 4" of 3,000 p.s.i. concrete. Then the sides are formed of 8" concrete blocks that are filled and strengthened with steel rods. The inside of the pond is then faced with 1" of cement that is painted with a double coat of light blue waterproof paint. Use only paint that is safe for fish. DO NOT USE SWIMMING POOL PAINT. Ask your dealer or buy it from a garden pond koi/goldfish specialist.

Hard and soft textures and regular and irregular outlines and materials are combined in this interesting waterfall-motif garden pool. Koi gather around the plants and also seek shade in the deeper section, which is closest to the waterfall and evergreens.

The sense of delicious coolness imparted by this overflowing pool is so powerful that it can almost be felt just from looking at the photo.

Your pet shop will have large variety of pond foods that are suitable for goldfish and koi. The best way to determine which is the best koi food is to test it. There are two tests that any individual can easily perform: the flotation test and the clouding water test. Using a large, clear drinking glass of warm water, add six to eight pellets. Measure how long they float, how long they stick together before they fall apart, and if all the pellets uniformly act the same or if some float and some sink.

After they have all dissolved or crumbled, shake the glass vigorously and allow the sediment to settle. See how clear the water is, for the clarity is disturbed only by soluble material contained in the pellets. The ideal food floats for a minimum of five minutes, sticks together when it falls to the bottom, and barely turns the water a very light yellow or tan. The author uses Wardley koi food because it has kept his fish alive for more than ten years.

Larger works on koi and/or goldfish go to great depths about how to build a pond for fishes, but they are basically useless except to give you an idea of how to build one to suit your own situation. My large koi book, *Koi of the World*, has photographs of some of Japan's most lovely ponds.

Feeding Your Koi

Koi are almost as omnivorous as people. They eat just about anything small enough to ingest. They don't have teeth in their outer jaws, but they do have them in their throats. They can't bite the hand that feeds them, but they can chew the food they swallow.

New-born koi require such small foods as infusoria, daphnia, and newly hatched brine shrimp. Infusoria and minute crustaceans exist by the millions in every outdoor pond, especially natural ones that are allowed to get a bit scruffy.

Older koi are best fed koi pellets that float. The flotation characteristic has two values: you see your fish eat so you know how much to feed them based upon how much they eat in a few minutes; and the pellets won't fall to the bottom and foul the water before the fish find them. The Japanese feed for color, and I find

A number of manufacturers have produced foods designed specifically for goldfish and koi, in various forms, including flakes and pellets. Compare prices and qualities and decide for yourself which you want to use. In any case, do NOT buy a brand of floating pellets made for mink or catfish. Goldfish and koi have food requirements very much different from those of mammals or even other fishes such as catfish.

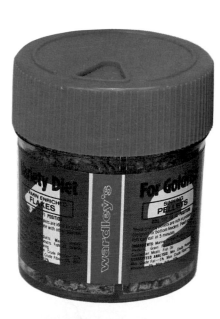

their recommendations comical. Mr. Kuroki, for example, recommends that you feed cabbage, watermelon, and green peppers. Please don't follow his advice! Stick with floating koi pellets available from almost every aquarium shop. If you are unable to get floating pellets, then feed something that does float, like small bits of bread. Variation in diet is very important for any caged animal like koi. Especially relished are minced clams that have been soaked and drained, as well as other small bits of shellfish. Freeze-dried foods available for aquarium fishes are great but expensive.

In general, feed your koi twice a day or more. Do not feed them heavily just once a day as they will be very hungry in the late afternoon, as evidenced by the way they greet you. The overfeeding in the morning only adds to tank pollution caused by the uneaten excess food.

To grow giant koi requires feeding almost every hour. Commercial fish breeders of koi, salmon, trout, and catfish have demand feeders that add food when the fishes demand it by either a signal to which the fishes are trained or some other mechanical means. Timed feeders are also available. These drop in small amounts of food in a pre-determined plan set on a clock.

Generally speaking, feed your fish in the morning before school or work and in the late afternoon when you return. During the

The water in this pond is so clear that the fish look like they are suspended in air. The pellets they are feeding upon all float for five minutes, giving the fish ample time to eat them before they fall apart and foul the shallow pond.

The koi in this large pond in Japan are fed everything the farmer can get his hands on from vegetables (like watermelon, I suppose) to silkworm cocoons. The cloudy water is a result of this poor feeding. The only way the koi farmer knows he still has fish is to feed them from one spot every day so they learn to congregate there and dash to the surface to feed.

winter when days are short, your fish will probably not eat at all. I have never seen a koi in an outdoor pond starve to death. I have seen thin ones, but never thin sickly ones. Perhaps the thin koi are healthier than their overfed brethren . . . much like humans!

Koi Diseases

The petshop in which you bought your koi probably has books about fish diseases. Perhaps if you contact your local wildlife and fisheries office or even the agricultural extension service, they can direct you to someone who can help you in controlling and preventing fish diseases. Koi are typical of most wild fishes and fall ill with the same diseases. You'll need experience, probably a microscope, and a desire to learn about fish diseases if you want to successfully control them in your koi pond. It is a lot easier to describe the disease to your petshop manager; he will sell you

77

Koi have thick skin and heavy scales, thus they are not likely to have many skin problems. Usually any discolored skin patch is a problem, and it usually takes a very low-powered microscope to ascertain the causative organism. Scrape a bit of the skin which appears affected onto a glass slide and examine it. The fish shown here has an epistylid infection—a protozoan growing on a scraped or cut area. Fish with most skin conditions require isolation and bathing in a very dilute solution of formaldehyde. Your pet shop should have books on fish diseases and parasites.

Some fish have "fish lice" (Argulus) that are fairly large (5 mm) and are easily seen with the naked eye. They can be removed with tweezers or, if many fish have them, treated with Dylox at a strength of 1 ppm.

Gill rot or columnaris disease is common and deadly in carp and koi. Various baths are suggested, especially potassium permanganate. It is best to consult a veterinarian or your pet shop owner. The gills of the infected fish lose their deep red color and are covered with slime. This is a very serious disease.

The carp above has an infection of anchor worms, parasitic copepods whose heads are buried in the skin and muscle with the egg sacs free in the water. The parasite is easily seen and treated. The fish below is infected with microscopic protozoans, myxosporidia, that are difficult to diagnose and impossible to effectively treat. Usually the gills are destroyed in young fish.

Ich (above) caused by the protozoan Ichthyophthirius *is familiar to all aquarists as "white spot disease." It is not common in koi unless they are stressed. Medications are available in any pet shop. Dropsy or raised scales, as in the koi below, is actually a symptom, not a disease. It can indicate anything from poor water, excess feeding, or internal injuries to bacterial diseases. Sometimes antibiotics will result in a cure, while other times just changing water conditions or feeding schedules will work.*

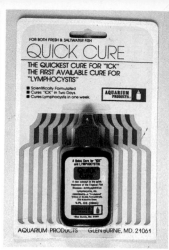

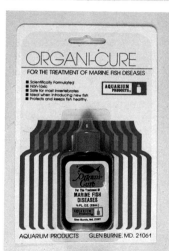

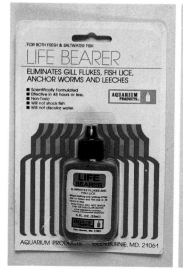

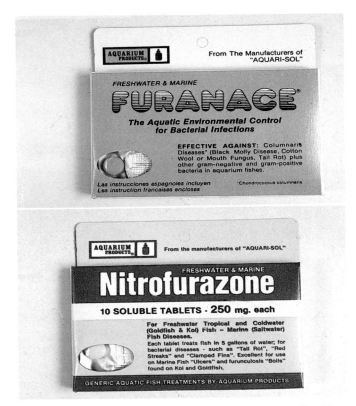

Your pet shop will be able to offer you many disease remedies. None of the remedies will be effective without a proper diagnosis of the disease causing the problem. A book on fish diseases is a necessary adjunct to every fish-lover's library. Your pet shop has such books.

some medicine that works in at least 50% of the cases. If it doesn't, then let nature take its course.

When fish as strong as koi get sick there is usually a water problem. Either the water is fouled and the fish are suffering from an oxygen shortage, or the pond is overcrowded. Koi need lots of oxygen. Green water (algal blooms), rotting food or plants on the bottom, and dull days when the plants give off carbon dioxide rather than oxygen can all make the pond go sour. Your first aid for an ailing koi pond is to immediately add fresh water. I

use a few garden hoses set on a fine mist spray (to aerate it) and spray the whole pool surface with mist. This misting also disperses the gaseous chlorine and fluorine content of the water.

The Japanese who have very valuable koi have koi doctors who vaccinate the fish against certain diseases and even perform surgery. Injections of antibiotics can be given intramuscularly or intravenously through a vein in the tail. Western koi-lovers are satisfied to add large quantities of antibiotics to hospital tanks containing sick koi.

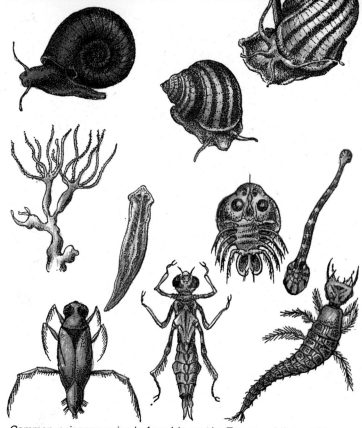

Common nuisance animals found in ponds: Top row, left to right: rams-horn snail, Japanese livebearing snails. Middle row, left to right: hydra, planaria, fish louse or Argulus, leech. Bottom row, left to right: water boat-man (predaceous bug), dragonfly nymph, larva of water beetle or water tiger.

Other Life in the Pond

If you are becoming interested in fish diseases, most of the diseases are caused or carried in by extraneous life in the ponds. The creatures living with your koi can be as large as snakes and turtles or so small that a powerful microscope is necessary to see them. Viruses even require an electron microscope for a close look. Pond life in itself can rival the koi in educational value, thus the inclusion of the following sections on typical pond life. This information is not available in any other koi, goldfish, or water garden book, and for that reason it has been done very elaborately. If you want more information about koi, ask your petshop to get a copy of *Koi of the World* for you to peruse. If you want more information about pond life, it doesn't exist (at the time of this writing) except in various more technical books about ecology and animal identification available at your library. These books dealing specifically with the infusoria, algae, snakes, turtles, and what have you of your own area are to be recommended to supplement the following generalizations.

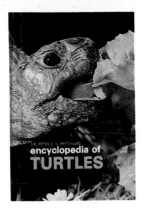

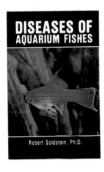

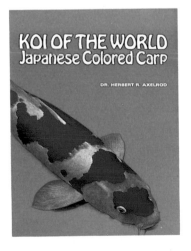

You cannot expect to be a successful fish hobbyist if you do not read. Books contain the answers to many of your problems and hints on how to prevent problems in the first place. They also contain fascinating background information on the fishes and other animals you see in your pet shop or that you find in your pond. Your pet shop sells many beautiful and useful books you should have in your library.

A

B

C

D

E

F

The Pond Flora

Seasonal Succession

In natural ponds, even though free water is present for only part of the year, there is a definite succession of living organisms. One species or a group of species will come, replacing another, only to be replaced in turn by something else. The drying of the pond or freezing of the entire basin of water will cause the death of many organisms and seems to serve as a "resting period" before the beginning of a new cycle of biotic events.

The successive use of the water by large concentrations of pond inhabitants makes for high productivity rates in relatively small areas. Populations of certain animals and plants at times get to almost unbelievable levels until something like dissolved carbon dioxide concentrations get so high as to completely eliminate the species.

Because of such factors as the presence of the excrement of water animals, most ponds are well fertilized and consequently can support a lush growth of plants. The vegetable tissues of the plants decompose during winter and, after thawing occurs,

serve indirectly as food for the aquatic animals.

Invertebrates emerge in large numbers from their resting sites in the soil on the bottom and become active almost immediately after spring rains. Animals such as the Entomostraca (copepods and daphnia) spend the resting period as eggs, while others, including the snails, rest as adults. As the season progresses, more species of algae are introduced and even some species of higher aquatic plants move in. In general, the number of species becomes greater as the season progresses.

Depending upon degree of illumination, natural ponds are either without plants or possess a vegetation that largely belongs to the land. Shallow depths allow sunlight to penetrate effectively to the bottom so that at times this vegetation may be abundant. Many of these aquatic plants are found in marshes and certainly could not be termed characteristic of ponds. Where these plants have been studied more carefully over yearly periods it was decided that those more commonly present seemed to come to flower over a much shorter period as they followed in rapid succession. Of course artificial ponds will have marginal plants and some floating vegetation.

Algae

Algae are most abundant in temporary waters, especially where there is much organic matter present. Populations of cellular and unicellular algae vary as the season progresses and should be examined with the use of a microscope both qualitatively and quantitatively.

Your pond or aquarium should contain plants. Larger plants are more desirable for ponds, but smaller plants are usually more attractive, grow better, and are suitable as spawning sites and baby hiders in the tanks. The plants illustrated and recommended for the pond or tank are: A) Hygrophila; *B)* Riccia, *a floating plant; C)* Azolla, *a floating plant; D)* Myriophylum *and* Cabomba; *E)* Ludwigia *and F)* Marsilea, *the four-leaf clover fern.*

Closterium crescents usually occur in new ponds that are heavily aerated and acid, with a pH between 5 and 6.

Single-celled green algae of the phylum Chlorophyta are sometimes found in sufficient numbers to color the water in temporary pools. Desmids usually occur as single cells but sometimes in the form of filaments or small colonies. They exhibit beautiful patterns of body form and may be found either freely floating or attached to objects in the water. As a rule, desmids reach their best development in small ponds, depending pretty much on the dissolved organic content. They are generally less than a hundredth of an inch in length.

Usually they are found in well aerated water that is low in carbon dioxide. Crescents of the larger species such as those of *Closterium* are typical of temporary ponds and can easily be seen with a hand lens. *Closterium* was described by Nitzsch in 1817. Cells are elongate, without a median constriction. There possibly is some correlation between abundance of the algae and pH. They seem to prefer water that is acid, with a pH varying between 5 and 6.

The differences between the approximately 65 species that occur in the United States are based on the general body shape, the amount of curvature of the crescent, the ornamentation of the cell wall, and the structure of the chloroplast.

Euastrum Ehrenberg, 1832, a generally small-celled but sometimes large-celled genus with an emarginate apical incision, differs from *Tetmemorus* in the marked compression of the semicells and in the different proportions between breadth and length.

Tetmemorus Rolfs, 1844, is an alga whose cells are fairly large and with a length two to eight times the breadth.

Micrasterias Agardh, 1827, has cells of a large size with a length somewhat greater than the breadth. The walls are generally unornamented, although a few species have rows of marginal spines or spines over the entire wall. There are approximately 35 species in this country.

Certain species of *Cosmarium* Corda, 1834, are difficult to distinguish from *Euastrum*. Most species have small, compressed cells with a length only slightly greater than the breadth and a deep median constriction. There

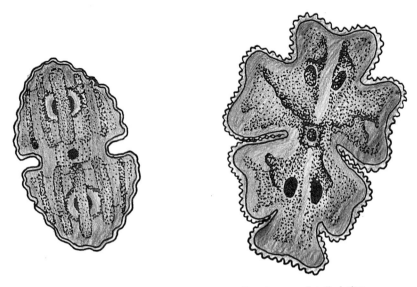

Euastrum *is a green desmid alga that occurs either in a small-celled size (left) or a large-celled size. They have many varied shapes.*

Tetmemorus *has a characteristic shape. Note that almost all algae are bilaterally symmetrical. That is, they can be sliced in half in such a way that each half is identical.*

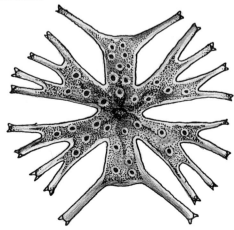

Micrasterias, *meaning "small star," is a beautiful alga. Microscopes are required to enjoy them.*

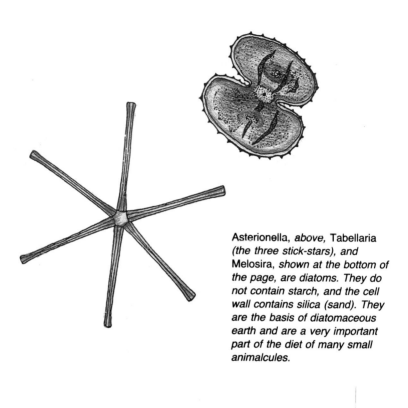

Asterionella, *above,* Tabellaria *(the three stick-stars), and* Melosira, *shown at the bottom of the page, are diatoms. They do not contain starch, and the cell wall contains silica (sand). They are the basis of diatomaceous earth and are a very important part of the diet of many small animalcules.*

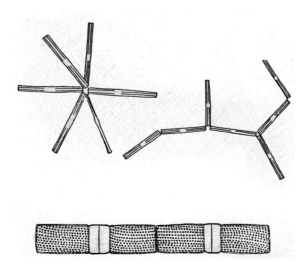

are approximately 245 species known in the United States.

It has been suggested by some limnologists that a low light intensity may be responsible for the rather large numbers of unicellular algae with yellow-brown chromatophores. The phylum Chrysophyta, which includes the diatoms *Asterionella*, *Tabellaria*, and *Melosira*, is rather well represented in temporary ponds, especially those in forested areas.

Starch is absent in the diatom cells, food substances being stored primarily as carbohydrates or as oils. Silica rather than cellulose is the major component of the cell walls. They are of prime importance as a basic food supply for small animals.

While living desmids are colored a bright green, living diatoms are golden yellow. Where large numbers are present, parts of the surface of ponds in early summer may glisten with gold. Some species are disc-shaped while others are boat-like or like spindles. They may be attached to each other end to end in a straight line or in the form of a zig-zag chain or possibly as a ring or star-shaped cluster.

Certain of the blue-green algae will become extremely abundant in ponds where the oxygen content is low and concentration of organic materials high. In other ponds where there is an abundance of carbon dioxide along with low oxygen content, but not excessive nitrogenous products, the algal flora will consist predominantly of filamentous and branched plants.

Spirogyra is typical of the filamentous algae sometimes found in ponds. It is usually found as a floating mat interlaced with bubbles of metabolic gases,

A messy, unsightly alga is Spirogyra, well known to every high school biology student. It is recognized microscopically by its spiraled chloroplast inside the cell. In unshaded still-water ponds it sometimes coats other plants and in general is an unsightly nuisance. It is hard to get rid of. Most alga-eating fishes, tadpoles, and the like graze on Spirogyra.

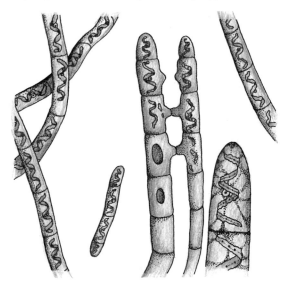

especially in sunny ponds. The alga is recognized by the typically spiraled chloroplast, though in some species fully mature fruiting material is essential for correct identification. This alga is often present in considerable quantity in ponds, especially those with exposure to direct sunlight.

Higher Aquatic Plants Higher aquatic plants are not very diverse in pond situations and usually are limited to those more tolerant species that are able to withstand freezing. In general, they are plants having heavy root-stocks that tend to creep throughout the entire pond basin.

The common cattail, *Typha latifolia* L., is sometimes present and may become very abundant in ponds and along the shores of lakes.

The bur-reed, *Sparganium eurycarpum* Engelm., or the giant

Spirogyra is a filamentous or mat alga. Although often a nuisance, large mats of this alga provide protection for fish fry and eggs.

bur-reed as it is sometimes called, is another marsh plant invading pond areas, where it may become very abundant.

The American water plantain, *Alisma subcordatum* Raf., is related to *A. plantago-aquatica* L. of the Old World and is found in ponds. It has broad heart-shaped leaves when growing marginally, but under water the leaves are ribbon-like. Adult syrphid flies feeding on pollen of the pyramidal clusters of small white flowers can be observed toward the end of a typical pond season.

The swamp buttercup, *Ranunculus septentrionalis* (L.) Poiret, is sometimes found about shaded pools. Actually this plant just happens to be one of the buttercups generally found in moist woodland areas, so it is not truly an aquatic plant.

If there are any aquatic plants which might be termed pond plants, they would be the purple-fringed riccia, *Ricciocarpus natans* (L.) Corda, and the crystalwort, *Riccia fluitans* L., which is sometimes called the slender riccia. Both of these plants float at the surface (the latter just below) of ponds and can adapt themselves to another type of habitat if the water evaporates and the plants are stranded on the muddy margins. A different type of growth occurs here.

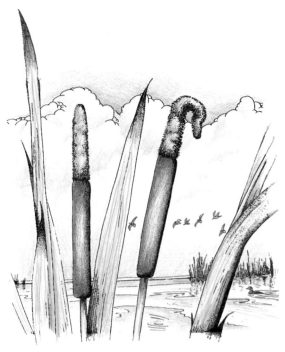

If your pond has a dirt bottom, it might maintain the common cattail, Typha, *shown at the top, or the giant bur-reed,* Sparganium, *shown at the bottom. These plants eventually invade standing water ponds.*

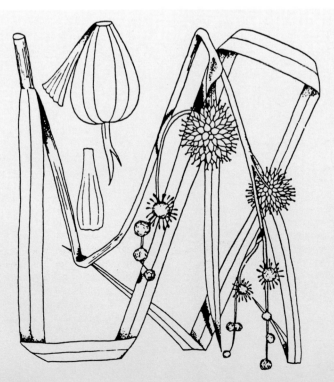

Crystalwort or Riccia looks like a floating green star, but it usually occurs in dense masses. Koi and goldfish sometimes eat them if they are hungry enough. They float and shade the bottom.

American water plantain, Alisma, is a welcome decoration to many ponds.

A syrphid fly, a common insect in pond-side plants.

The swamp buttercup, Ranunculus, *is often sold as an aquarium plant. Below is another type of riccia, the purple-fringed* Ricciocarpus.

The Pond Fauna

Faunal Characteristics

The reproductive potential of ponds, as observed repeatedly, is very high because of a pond's amazing ability to re-populate itself. Some animals found in the pond get there by accident from other places and really are not typical. There are many, however, that are characteristic.

Ponds serve as refuges, feeding sites, and as breeding places for a variety of animals. If the pond dries back, some animals die for lack of moisture, others assume a resting condition, while others migrate to deeper areas where water still exists.

Among the vertebrates, amphibians constitute the most conspicuous group, but the pool plankton consists largely of minute crustaceans carried in by the wind or floods or introduced on the bodies of the invading amphibia and on the feet of birds. Populations vary among pools depending upon whether or not they have a clean hard bottom or an accumulation of sediment.

Protozoa

Even in the very coldest days of winter, single-celled animals can be found swimming about freely, attached to the stones and debris on the bottom, or attached to the other larger animals swimming about. As the season progresses, quantities of the various species increase tremendously, often coloring the water shades of green and red. Ponds are sources of vast numbers of protozoans, but only a few can be seen without the aid of a microscope.

The "slipper-shaped" rapidly swimming *Paramecium* thrives in debris-filled pools of water in the early spring along with countless other Protozoa. They feed on the bacteria of organic wastes or directly on the waste material itself. They can actually be identified by observing their smooth and spiral-like swimming movements through the water. A clean, wide-mouth glass test tube is all that is necessary to draw in enough water close to the shoreline and observe the

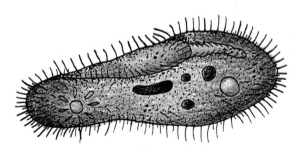

Typical Paramecium. *These small animals are necessary for feeding small, newborn fishes.*

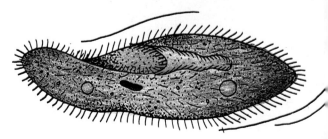

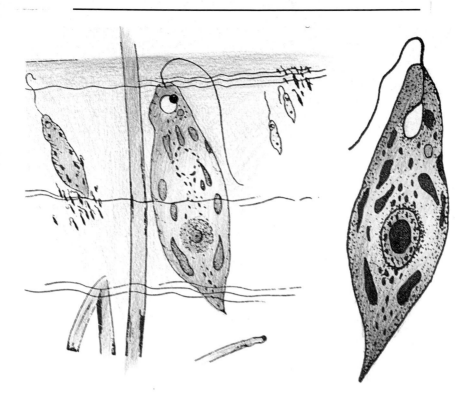

Euglena *(above) is another small animal that, like* Spirostomum *(below), is necessary as a first food for fry of many egg-laying fishes. Naturally, microscopes are necessary to see and identify these little single-celled animals.*

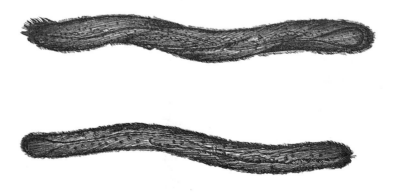

Protozoa swimming about. Of course it is necessary to hold the tube up in order to get proper background lighting.

When present in very large numbers, *Euglena* may appear as a green film on the surface of the water or collectively as a green cloud in sunny parts of the pool. Resting cysts may "paint" the bottom mud with conspicuous green spots. *Euglena* serve as an excellent food for larger organisms. *Euglena spirogyra* is found close to shore in mud holes filled with decomposing organic matter. It is beautifully colored, easy to see, and much larger than *E. viridis* but not nearly as numerous.

Spirostomum can be found among fallen tree leaves that are undergoing decomposition and might even be giving off a few bubbles of hydrogen sulfide. They are also found in sunny open spots, but usually only in those where there is an abundance of decaying vegetation. During the day *Spirostomum* takes over beneath the submerged leaves and mats of debris, but at night it swims about freely. Although it is usually less than a tenth of an inch in length, to the naked eye this tiny protozoan appears long and slim and somewhat flattened on its sides as it swims through the water. Sometimes in the early morning, large numbers of the animal may actually whiten the surface of shallow pond margins.

Whenever *Stentor* are disturbed, they retreat hurriedly to the bottom of their pools. They are so very changeable in form that when swimming they look almost like microscopic whales, but as soon as they attach themselves to some object in the water, they blossom out as beautiful trumpets. *Stentor* range in color from entirely colorless to a brilliant blue. Two common species are *S. coeruleus* Ehrenberg and *S. polymorphus* (Muller).

Vorticella can be found in temporary pools covering portions of the bottom or attached to floating bits of debris, sometimes resembling a cotton covering or little spots of white slime or mucus. The bodies of water insects and various crustacea such as *Daphnia* are often covered with *Vorticella*. Usually they are observed as clusters, but with a little experience they can be seen as individuals. Their actual numbers seem to be directly proportional to the amount of organic matter present in the water. The food particles utilized by the protozoan consist mostly of bacteria swept in through the mouth and into the gullet. In the very early spring rotifers have been observed

Stentor *is a very interesting animalcule and is a popular aquarium food for hatching fry. They are sometimes colored a nice blue. They only have the trumpet shape when attached.*

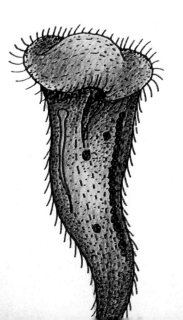

Vorticella, *the bell animalcule, is a great fish food for small fish. They cannot move on their own very well, but they often attach to swimming crustaceans like daphnia, the water flea.*

feeding rather extensively on the clusters.

Ponds are sometimes literally filled with *Volvox* so they often tint the water a bright green. To the naked eye they can be seen as tiny green balls rolling smoothly through the water. Two of the most common species are *V. globator* L. and *V. aureus* Ehr. Botanists and zoologists differ in opinion as to how *Volvox* should be classified taxonomically:

	Botanically	**Zoologically**
PHYLUM	Chlorophyta	Protozoa
CLASS	Chlorophyceae	Mastigophora
ORDER	Volvocales	Phytomonadina
FAMILY	Volvocaceae	Volvocidae
GENUS	*Volvox*	*Volvox*

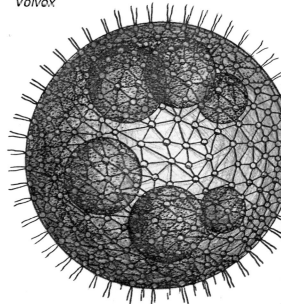

Volvox, *a colonial animalcule, is sometimes listed as an alga since it contains the green pigment chlorophyl. Scientists still argue about those living things that cross borders between the plant and animal worlds. The smaller the living thing gets, the harder it is to classify.*

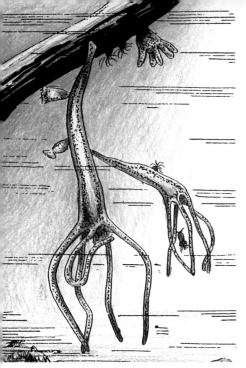

They can be seen dangling their tentacles into the water, often almost an inch long, or contracted into a ball as small as a pinhead.

Planaria Flatworms glide on the surface of debris and on the bottoms of the ponds. The little black, brown, or white worms often take in whole animals through a mouth that is halfway down the body on the underside. *Hymanella retenuova* Castle is grayish in color with darkly pigmented eyespots near the anterior end. Auricles (side-protruberances at the anterior end) are present but not always prominent. *Phagocata vernalis* Kenk is an elongated species tapering posteriorly and with two normal eyes. Color varies from white to a dark gray. The worms are very active in the winter under the ice and throughout spring.

Rotifers Often tiny rotifers become so abundant and are so

Hydra are fearsome animals that attach themselves to the wall of an aquarium or pond debris and feed upon passing small fish fry or daphnia. The tentacles are poisonous, and they snare the hapless prey.

Hydra Almost certainly, wherever daphnids appear in large numbers, hydra are apt to be there too, and this generally applies to ponds as well. Sometimes they increase in numbers so rapidly as to eliminate their food supply, and then they decrease rapidly as well. *Cyclops, Cypris*, and minute worms also are eaten ravenously by hydra. Aquarists have to keep them out of their fish-breeding tanks if they expect to have any fish at all to raise to maturity. The common species are *Chlorohydra viridissima* (Pallas), the green hydra; *Hydra americana* Hyman, the white hydra; and *H. oligactis* (Pallas), the true brown hydra.

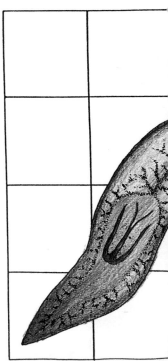

100

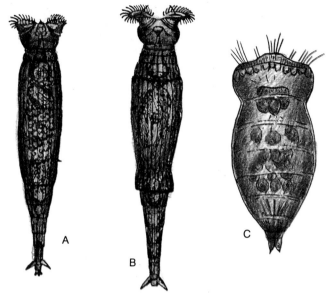

The best foods for newborn fry are rotifers. Shown are A) Philodina; B) Rotifer; and C) Hydatina. These microscopic animals can be (and should be) cultured for feeding to young fishes. Aquarists who spawn goldfish and koi in tanks or temporary plastic containers should have these small animals available for feeding the newly hatched fry. There is a wonderful book about "live foods" that tells you how to culture and recognize many of these animals.

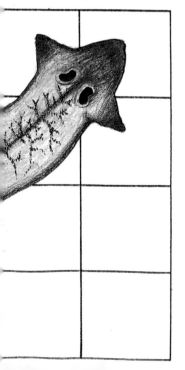

brightly colored that they give the pond a tinge of their very own color. In places where dissolved organic matter is usually in abundance there is apt to be a large number of individuals represented by only a few species. The ciliated area near the anterior end of the body, which serves as a means of bringing food into the mouth and also serves as a locomotor organ, is probably the most characteristic feature of the rotifers. Common vernal pool species are *Philodina roseola* Ehr., *Rotifer citrinus* Ehr., and

Flatworms (as contrasted to round worms) are just that . . . flat. They may have side protuberances or they may not. They are eaten by many species of fish and refused by others.

101

The polluted pond is often laden with bryozoans or moss animals, such as Plumatella *shown above.*

Hydatina senta Ehr. Although the same size as many protozoans, rotifers are quite advanced multicellular animals with the normal organ systems found in most invertebrates. Their closest relatives probably are the roundworms.

Bryozoans The moss animals, bryozoans, are represented best by *Plumatella*. Sunken logs, twigs, rocks and old leaves on the bottom very often have delicate traceries of these animals on their undersides. Usually they appear as transparent (or brown) branching tubes which trail vine-like. Very rarely are they found in highly polluted waters or where the dissolved oxygen content is low. By virtue of their resistant statoblasts (resting cells), bryozoans are one of the few larger freshwater animals capable of withstanding transport overland on the feet of water birds, turtles, and frogs.

Also common are the large jelly-like colonies of *Pectinatella*. Smaller colonies look like globs of brownish jelly or twigs, but large colonies a foot or more in diameter are often seen. These usually disintegrate into real blobs of jelly with the coming of autumn.

Bristleworms
The oligochaetes or bristleworms (aquatic earthworms) are well represented in most ponds. Their diet consists of decayed organic matter either on the bottom or as floating masses on the surface. Bristleworms serve well as agents for cleaning up unwanted debris. Because of the fact that the body wall of the worms is so thin and so very well supplied with capillaries, an exchange of respiratory gases takes place through the integument. Some of the species can stand quite a deficiency in dissolved oxygen.

The following types are often found in ponds:
Purely aquatic
1. Aeolosomatidae (spotted worms)
2. Naididae (the naids)
3. Tubificidae (tubificids)
Semi-aquatic (edges)
4. Lumbriculidae (small red or brown earthworms that live in very wet mud)
5. Haplotaxidae (thread annelids)
6. Enchytraeidae (white worms)

Crustacea Crustacea are probably the animals most typical of ponds. The eggs of some not only will stand drying out, but

actually require that they be dried and even frozen before they will hatch. It has been shown that the eggs can withstand very long periods of desiccation often overlapping several seasons. They may be grouped as follows: ENTOMOSTRACA (small, often minute)

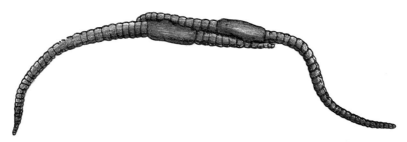

Enchytraeus, *a white worm, is one of the best foods for discus, one of the most sought-after of aquarium fishes. They are easily cultured. See the book* Encyclopedia of Live Foods, *available at your pet shop.*

The Pond Fauna

*Branchiopods, or fairy shrimp,
are excellent fish foods. Their
eggs can be stored in the freezer
and hatched years later.*

1. Branchiopoda
   —Fairy Shrimps
2. Cladocera
   —*Daphnia* and other daphnids
3. Copepoda
   —*Cyclops, Diaptomus* and
   other copepods
4. Ostracoda
   —*Cypris* and other ostracods
   MALACOSTRACA (larger)
5. Amphipoda
   —Scuds, *Gammarus* and
   Hyalella
6. Isopoda
   —Sowbugs, *Asellus*
7. Decapoda
   —Crayfishes, *Cambarus* and
   allies

FAIRY SHRIMP
   Eubranchipus vernalis Verrill is
a characteristic animal of
temporary pools. In fact, it occurs
almost exclusively in that habitat
because it is so very well adapted
to the environmental properties of
just such a body of water. The
eggs survive in the dry soil, hot in
summer and cold in winter for
many long months, then
development and reproduction
occur in a short time during late
winter and spring while water is
present.
   Fairy shrimp are the largest of
the entomostracans, usually
about an inch long, although

some report collecting much
larger specimens. They swim
about on their backs with their
gill-feet held upward. Their bodies
are semi-transparent with
greenish and pinkish colorations.
Populations vary tremendously in
pools from year to year.
Maximum counts can generally
be made within a week or two
after the ice melts in the spring,
when some adults already are
falling to the bottom and dying.
Sometimes their lives are
lengthened by prolonged cold
spells. Fairy shrimp have been
observed completely covered with
attached Protozoa and green
algae, causing them to swim
about with extreme difficulty.
They are practically defenseless
against the predations of aquatic
insects, but other enemies such
as frogs also take their toll.

DAPHNIDS
   Daphnia and its relatives are
certainly not confined to ponds,
but in such places they do make
up the bulk of the animal "flesh."
In very early spring, under ice,
relatively few daphnids are to be
found, but as soon as the water
temperature reaches six to twelve
degrees above freezing, active
reproduction begins and
subsequently increases

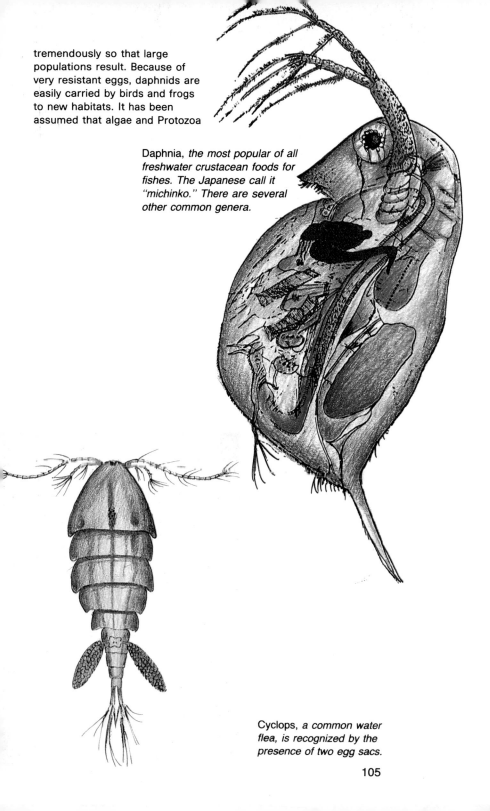

tremendously so that large populations result. Because of very resistant eggs, daphnids are easily carried by birds and frogs to new habitats. It has been assumed that algae and Protozoa

Daphnia, *the most popular of all freshwater crustacean foods for fishes. The Japanese call it "michinko." There are several other common genera.*

Cyclops, *a common water flea, is recognized by the presence of two egg sacs.*

serve chiefly as food, but now it is well known that organic detritus of all kinds, as well as bacteria, are very important in the diet of these water fleas. Common species are *Daphnia pulex* (DeGeer) and *Daphnia magna* Straus (much larger one) as well as numerous other species of allied genera such as *Bosmina*.

CYCLOPS

In general, *Cyclops* and related copepods are much more tolerant of oxygen deficiencies than are other water fleas. Even when only an extremely small amount of water is present they can be seen jerking about. The females with two egg sacs are commonly observed. *Cyclops* passes through periods of activity and rest as do the other small crustaceans. Their legs are free for swimming purposes but they still use their antennae for help in moving about.

DIAPTOMUS

Unlike the female *Cyclops*, *Diaptomus* has but one egg sac. The exceptionally long straight antennae also are distinguishing characteristics. They filter the surrounding water in search of food by means of flickering structures moving back and forth about their mouth. Organic debris suspended in the water as well as single-celled algae and Protozoa serve as food. In some cases the integument may be deeply colored in reds, blues, and purples caused by oil globules accumulated as reserve food. Ponds frequently swarm with the individuals of only a few, sometimes but one, species. They usually swim but occasionally crawl or run about the bottom.

CYPRIS

Cypris resemble microscopic clams in having a pair of shells that swing on hinges and close by using muscles. In fact, an old European name for this animal was mussel shrimp. In the United States, the name seed shrimp is a more common one. They are technically called ostracods. They clamber over the bottoms and debris of ponds in extremely large numbers by means of a movement that has been described as creeping, uncertain, weak, tottering, rapid, bouncing, or scurrying. Although a filter feeder, it can also pull large food particles directly into its shell. *Cypris* are scavengers and can be seen feeding vigorously on decomposing grass and leaves.

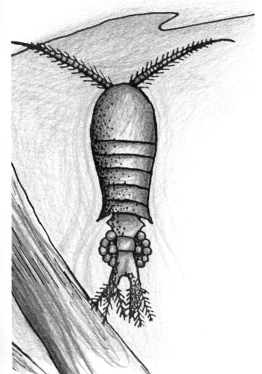

Diaptomus, *closely related to* Cyclops, *is often mistaken for* Cyclops *but it only has one egg sac.*

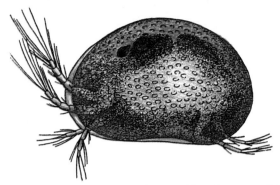

Cypris is a crustacean that looks like a clam. They have two shells and move about fairly well, feeding on decaying vegetation.

SCUDS

Scuds are usually abundant in temporary pools feeding on the accumulated vegetable matter, but not if there is a deficiency of dissolved oxygen. Like crayfishes, scuds often are found with a heavy covering of algae and Protozoa over their entire body. Usually the animals feed on vegetable matter directly, but they can sometimes be seen browsing on the film of microscopic plants and animals covering leaves, stems, and bottoms of temporary pools. Occasionally they will rapidly consume small freshly killed animals. Birds, fishes, aquatic insects, and frogs and toads feed eagerly on scuds. The common species are *Gammarus limnaeus* Smith and *G. fasciatus* Say, as well as the spiny-backed *Hyalella azteca.*

Scuds, Gammarus, *are wonderful aquarium fish foods and should be cultured more often.*

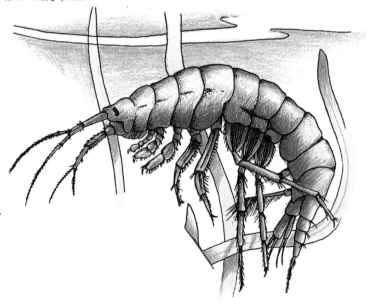

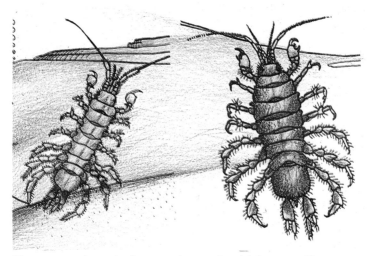

The water sowbugs, Asellus, *are slow-moving debris eaters. They usually are not plentiful in the koi pond, one reason being that they are heavily preyed upon by other animals in the pond. Koi will eat* Asellus, *but these crustaceans never are a major part of their diet.*

WATER SOWBUGS

Asellus species are especially abundant on leaf-filled pool bottoms where the water is acidic and aquatic insects are scarce. Sowbugs crawl about sluggishly feeding on the mass of litter on the bottom, both plant and animal, and are also found among moist grass and leaves close to shore. There seems to be a direct correlation between the presence of calcium in the water and *Asellus*. The color is a grayish brown.

CRAYFISHES

Burrowing forms of crayfish delight in making their "homes" in moist depressions no matter where they may occur. *Cambarus diogenes* Girard occurs in meadows and pond margins over much of the eastern United States. Very often the chimneys

of the crayfish can be found scattered about the edges of such places. The chimneys are usually about 6 inches high (sometimes over 12 inches) and are constructed only at night. Except during the breeding season, each burrow houses a single crayfish. The purpose of the chimney is still uncertain, but the animal certainly seeks moist seclusion here and disposes of the mud pellets in this most convenient way.

In the southern United States almost any pond will soon be occupied by crayfishes of the genus *Procambarus*. Although most species feed on detritus, some actively attack small fishes. There are about 300 species of crayfishes in the United States and Mexico, with new species being described each year.

Mites Rapidly swimming mites, like tiny bright red spiders, are exciting to see in ponds. They are especially abundant as the pool gets older during its season, but they can be seen even under ice. Those forming the order Hydracarina are one of the few characteristic freshwater groups, being almost restricted to fresh

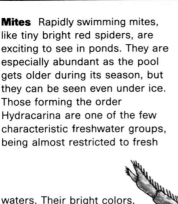

waters. Their bright colors, globular to ovoid shape, and clambering-swimming habits easily identify them. Some of the

genera are *Thyas, Hydryphantes, Acercus, Piona,* and *Limnesia.* All are quite capable of withstanding periods of hardship by burrowing in wet soil and debris.

Aquatic Insects Many insects are adapted to complete the larval part of their life cycle in ponds. Others fly in just to feed on the rich populations of food animals while they are available, then move on to other locations. Most are so very active that they need large amounts of oxygen and take it by means of breathing tubes, even while living in the water. Some of the insects most annoying to man, such as the mosquitoes, lay their eggs on the water's surface or along the wet shorelines and live there while young. Most common pond insects fall in the following orders:
Collembola—Springtails
Hemiptera—
    Water Scorpion (True Bugs)
Trichoptera—Caddisflies
Coleoptera—Beetles

Crayfishes are enemies of koi. Small fish traps usually trap the crayfish as well so they can be removed.

Diptera
   —Flies (Mosquitoes, Midges)

SPRINGTAILS
   On the surface of ponds, springtails collect in great patches often resembling floating

109

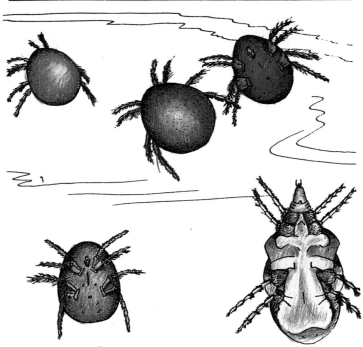

These aquatic mites are very common if the fish don't eat them. They are free-swimming and look like miniature spiders. Occasionally they are found on fishes, but they don't seem to harm koi in any way.

soot. They can sometimes be found in the very early spring even when ice and snow are present. Their small size and water-repellent body surface prevent them from breaking through the surface film. If disturbed, springtails leap high into the air in all directions like an erupting spray. This jumping movement is accomplished by forcing a spring-like appendage suddenly downward. They feed chiefly on algae, other plant tissues, and vegetable debris of all kinds.

WATER SCORPIONS

Looking very much like some of the brown stems or twigs submerged in the clear water of ponds can be found water scorpions, *Ranatra fusca* Beauvois, crawling about. They

A springtail. Large groups of springtails are commonly found on shallow water in koi ponds.

are some of the flying insects moving in from some adjacent pond just to take advantage of the big crop of *Daphnia*. They hang head downward with air tubes thrust up to the surface. Length of the adult varies from 1 to 1¼ inches. The insect is not content with a steady diet of water fleas but instead will feed heavily on such animals as tadpoles and even snails. Because of their slow movements and protective morphology and coloration they can sometimes be difficult to see.

Many other true bugs are found in ponds, and many feed on fish fry if they get the chance.

CADDISFLY LARVAE

Some species of caddisflies estivate in the accumulated debris of ponds during short periods of dryness such as may occur in the hot summer months. None, however, could be called typical pond species. Caddisflies are best known because of their larvae (stickworms) that crawl about cautiously over and through leaves and vegetable trash in search of small crustaceans and annelids. There seems to be a preference for waters in which there is much dissolved oxygen. The adults do not venture far from their water homes and are usually seen at dusk or night around close-by lights. They look like small moths with very long antennae.

Water scorpions can kill small koi fry. They also eat daphnia, Cyclops, and other small living things in a koi pond. They look like floating sticks.

GREAT DIVING BEETLE

In ponds the larva of this aquatic beetle is known as the water tiger. Aquarists who gather large quantities of living *Daphnia* almost invariably pick up a tiger or two in their collection. Sometimes they're hard to see among all the other actively moving animals, but they have to be kept out of an aquarium or small pond if the fish are to be saved. Both adults and larvae are highly predaceous and feed upon a variety of small aquatic animals. The adults may leave the pools at night seeking out other places to take over. Adults obtain air at the surface of the water and carry it trapped in a chamber under the elytra (outer wings) so they can stay submerged long periods.

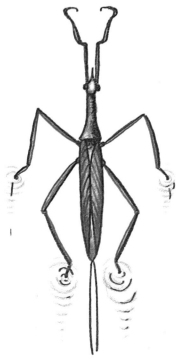

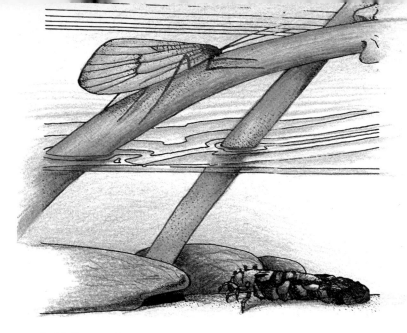

Caddisflies are found around every pond at night. These small moth-like insects have larvae that live in the koi pond. They are neither a menace nor an asset.

Water beetles, both adults and larvae, must be kept out of the pond-and the aquarium. They feed on small fishes and small insects. If you see the adult on the surface, try to net it out.

Bloodworms (above) are sold as fish foods mostly in eastern Europe, but they are almost universally available if you want to collect them. They are excellent fish foods. Dixa (below) is the larva of another type of midge; the adults look and act like non-biting mosquitoes.

BLOODWORMS

The larvae of the Chironomidae (midges) are known best as "bloodworms" because of hemoglobin contained within their bright red bodies. The insect's short life cycle, lasting but five or six weeks, makes it possible for several generations to be raised each season. Eggs are laid early in spring as gelatinous globules on leaves and debris just under water close to shore. From then on during the spring and early summer the size of the "worms" in the pools varies from one-eighth inch to one inch depending upon species and age. In some pools large larvae can be collected in huge quantities under ice during the winter time. They are frequently sold as fish food in pet shops.

DIXID MIDGES

In ponds *Dixa* feed primarily on algal cells at the surface of the water much like mosquito larvae, but the usual position is with the body bent into a **U** with the head and tail close together. Sometimes the larvae can be found on debris above the water level but in the surface film.

Another available aquarium fish food is Corethrella, *a glassworm.*

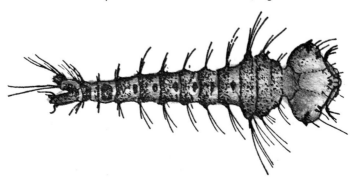

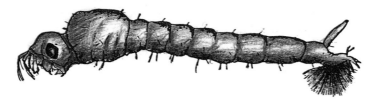

Mochlonyx *is another genus of the glassworm group that aquarists prize as excellent fish food.*

Antennae of the larvae are simple. Mouth brushes are present and composed of numerous hairs. Eggs are laid in masses of jelly. Adults are small, long-legged, and quite mosquito-like but they do not bite. Scales are lacking on the wings.

GLASSWORMS

The virtually transparent larvae of these mosquito-like midges (family Chaoboridae) are usually found near the surface. The adults look like very delicate pale mosquitoes. Only a few genera are common.

Corethrella is found in pools, but not too much is known about its egg-laying habits. The larvae are reddish in color and rather small. Adults are less than 2 mm in length. Very young larvae of *Mochlonyx* are found in woodland pools in the early spring, indicating that the insect probably overwinters either as an egg or as an adult. Eggs are deposited singly on the surface of the water, and the developing larvae feed voraciously on early mosquito wrigglers, small crustaceans, and

other minute forms of animal life. *Eucorethra* is extremely widespread throughout pools of northern United States and Canada. Not too much is known about their biology except that they have been observed in the very early spring feeding voraciously on mosquito larvae of the genus *Aedes*.

The larvae of *Chaoborus* are commonly called ghost larvae, glassworms, or phantom midges because they are so transparent one can hardly see them floating horizontally in the water. In fact, if it weren't for their black eyes and silvery air sacs, even though they may be a half-inch long they'd be invisible. *Chaoborus* larvae can be extremely abundant in ponds, feeding heavily on small crustaceans and insects. Their structure and peculiar habits offer much to the research biologist. *Chaoborus* live where there is plenty of shade and organic matter. They hide from the bright day sun in the soft bottom ooze. Low oxygen, high CO_2 content, and even some H_2S are characteristics of the pools where *Chaoborus* can be found in abundance. They are often sold in petshops as fish food.

MOSQUITOES

The larvae usually hang from

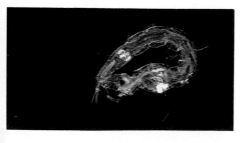

Ghost larvae or glassworms, Chaoborus, *make excellent fish food.*

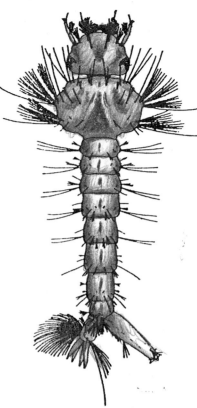

the film on the surface of the water and take in air by means of breathing tubes. Feeding is accomplished by moving two large feeding brushes on the head so as to make a current from which food particles are removed. Adult mosquitoes from temporary pools are often parasitized by hydrachnid mites and often have several attached to them as they fly about. Occasionally the larvae

Mosquito larvae can be frozen in small tubes of water for later use.

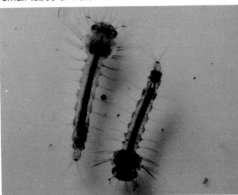

Aedes, *a mosquito, shown as a larva.*

The tail end of a Culiseta *mosquito larva showing the basal tuft on the breathing tube.*

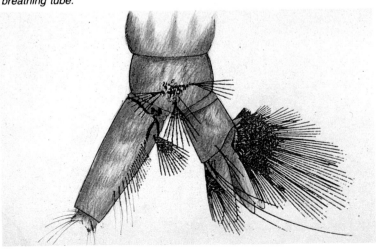

The slug Agriolimax *is a slimy animal that is not eaten by most animals unless that animal is very hungry.*

will be infected. The eggs of *Aedes* Meigen are laid on moist soil or humus in low places that are subject to filling with rain or snow. The eggs of *Culiseta* Felt and *Culex* Linnaeus are fixed together in boat-shaped rafts.

Tadpole Snail Living snails usually appear almost as soon as the ponds thaw out in the early

spring. *Physa gyrina* Say rarely reaches an overall length of three-fourths of an inch. Its body is colored yellowish gray or somewhat darker. The snails may have been carried into the pond from other ponds by flood waters or on the feet of frogs, turtles, or even birds. They are sometimes found in pools choked up with plant debris or even where the water may be polluted.

Frogs and Toads Frogs and toads use pond waters as places in which to breed. They spend most of the time away from water but come back in the spring to

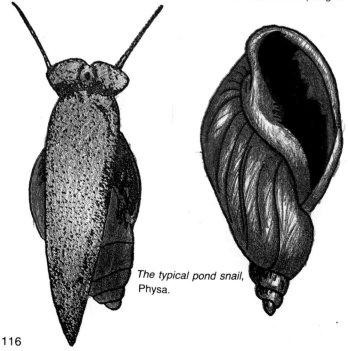

The typical pond snail, Physa.

Most tadpoles look much alike, differing only in color from species to species. They are aquatic and feed mostly on algae. As they slowly metamorphose, they change from tadpoles to frogs. Frogs breathe air.

The natterjack toad of Europe.

The American toad, Bufo americanus, *in a breeding embrace (above). Below is the spring peeper,* Hyla crucifer.

mate and lay their eggs. The more truly aquatic frogs make their homes in the more permanent ponds and lakes, whereas those species with relatively short aquatic stages in their life histories visit ponds for only a short while. Some of the aquatic species lay their eggs by the thousands in ponds.

moist without going into the water.

Tree frogs (*Hyla*) lay their eggs in small masses on the surface of quiet temporary ponds and attach them to debris or vegetation. Development is rapid, and the tadpoles soon can be seen darting around leaf-filled areas. They move about almost as

The green frog, Rana clamitans melanota.

Toads *(Bufo)* are found breeding early in spring. Their eggs are laid in long strings of jelly close to shore and sometimes exposed to the drying winds. It isn't long before hatching occurs and the young toads, one-half inch in length, leave the water to fatten up on insects. During the hot sunny days adults can be found in the cool shade under boards and stones trying to keep their skin

rapidly as fishes, certainly not in the typical "polywog" manner. The rest of the year the tree frogs live under the roots of trees and under leaves or perched on the bark of large tree trunks. In the evening they can be seen and heard moving about the branches of trees.

The spring peeper is a small relative of the tree frog (*Hyla crucifer*). They are usually the first frogs heard in the spring in the northeastern United States, often coming out of hibernation in February or March on mild days. Males can be seen on bushes about pools with their throats looking much like inflated

119

Hyla, *like the green tree frog* (Hyla cinerea) *shown above, lay their eggs in water.*

balloons. They feed on mosquitoes, gnats, small flies and beetles. Other frogs and snakes prey upon them as they dart swiftly about the shoreline bushes and trees.

At least a few true frogs (*Rana*) are likely to call at your pond each year to breed or hunt. The most common eastern United States species are the grass frog (*R. pipiens*), green frog (*R. clamitans*), and bull frog (*R. catesbeiana*).

WATER SNAKES

The common water snakes (*Nerodia*), like so many other animals, come to ponds to feed on the great variety and great number of animal forms present. Night and day they glide through the water and along the shoreline, picking up frogs and all sorts of living things. They are never found far from water. The young may be brilliantly marked, but as they grow older they tend to darken so that the pattern becomes obscure, at least in many common species.

TURTLES

Because they are so very widely distributed and common in most localities, any turtle to be found in temporary pools is quite apt to be a Painted Turtle that has just come over for a visit, the temptation of so much good food

The northern watersnake, Nerodia sipedon, *eats small fishes and frogs and is not friendly to humans, either. If you find one in your pond, do not handle it. Catch it in a net and return it to the nearest stream.*

Ambystoma maculatum *is an eastern American salamander that is often collected as a terrarium animal.*

Pseudemys scripta *was once the most popular of the pet turtles and was cultured in tremendous numbers. They can be kept in a koi pond.*

being hard to pass up. *Chrysemys picta* is the single species.

In the southern United States sliders (*Pseudemys*) somewhat replace painted turtles and are very likely to move into a pond. Most eat fish as well as plants and invertebrates. Even box turtles (*Terrapene*) may wander in during the heat of the summer or in late fall to pass some time during the heat or cold buried in the mud.

Further Reading

The following T.F.H. books deal in greater depth with koi, garden ponds and the plants and animals likely to be found with them. Most are available at your local pet shop. As your interest in koi and garden ponds increases, you will find them fascinating and useful references to help you learn more about the little world that lives in your back yard.

Axelrod, H.R. *Koi of the World,* 240 pages. H-947.

Axelrod, H.R. and W. Vorderwinkler. *Goldfish and Koi in Your Home.* 224 pages. H-909.

Axelrod, H.R., et al. *Dr. Axelrod's Atlas of Freshwater Aquarium Fishes.* 782 pages. H-1077.

Breen, J.F. *Encyclopedia of Reptiles and Amphibians.* 576 pages. H-935.

Goldstein, R.J. *Diseases of Aquarium Fishes.* 128 pagese. PS-201.

Hoffman, G.L. and F. Meyer. *Parasites of Freshwater Fishes.* 244 pages. PS-208.

Jocher, W. *Turtles for Home and Garden.* 128 pages. PS-307.

Leetz, T. *The T.F.H. Book of Snakes.* 96 pages. HP-017.

Matsui, Y. *Goldfish Guide.* 256 pages. PL-2011.

Post, G. *Textbook of Fish Health.* 256 pages. H-1043.

Pritchard, P.C.H. *Encyclopedia of Turtles.* 896 pages. H-1011.

Rataj, K and T. Horeman. *Aquarium Plants.* 448 pages. H-966.

Schubert, G. *Cure and Recognize Aquarium Fish Diseases.* 128 pages. PS-210.

Stetson, P. *Garden Pools.* 64 pages. M-513.

Takeshita, G.Y. *Koi for Home and Garden.* 96 pages. PS-659.

Thomas, G.L., Jr. *Goldfish Pools, Water Lilies and Tropical Fishes.* 336 pages. H-919.

Weiss, W. *Aquarium Keeping . . . Easy as ABC.* 96 pages. PS-831.

Zimmermann, E. *Breeding Terrarium Animals.* 384 pages. H-1078.

turtles for home and garden

willy jocher

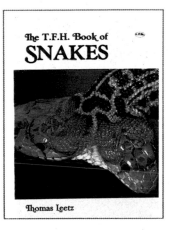

The T.F.H. Book of SNAKES

Thomas Leetz

TEXTBOOK OF FISH HEALTH

DR. GEORGE W. POST

Index

Magnificent French goldfish/koi ponds painted by Monet at Giverny. These paintings decorate the front and back endpages.

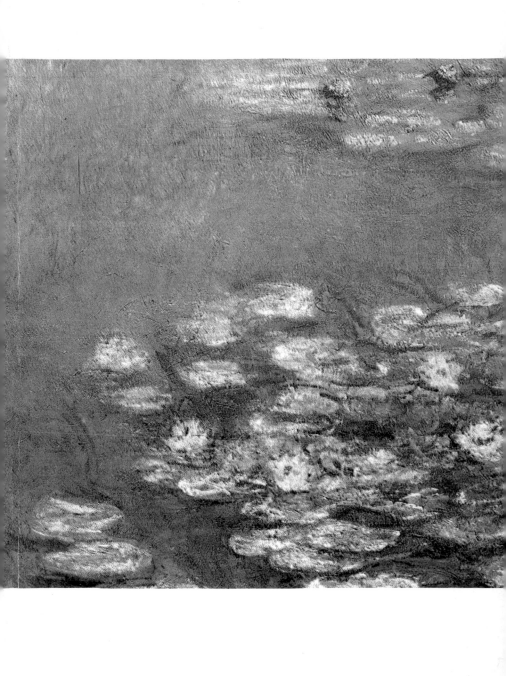